Praise for the *Roots of Contemporary Issues series*

"Everything around us—policy, population, culture, economy, environment—is a product of the actions and activities of people in the past. How can we hope to address the challenges we face and resolve contentious issues—like inequality, health, immigration, and climate change—without understanding where they come from? The volumes in the Roots of Contemporary Issues series are the tested products of years of classroom teaching and research. They address controversial issues with impartiality but not detachment, combining historical context and human agency to create accounts that are meaningful and usable for any student confronting the complex world in which they will live."

—TREVOR R. GETZ, *San Francisco State University*

"This is a truly innovative series that promises to revolutionize how world history is taught, freeing students and faculty alike from the 'tyranny of coverage' often embedded within civilizational paradigms, and facilitating sustained reflection on the roots of the most pressing issues in our contemporary world. Students' understanding of the importance of history and their interest in our discipline is sure to be heightened by these volumes that deeply contextualize and historicize current global problems."

—NICOLA FOOTE, *Arizona State University*

ROOTS OF CONTEMPORARY ISSUES

POWER POLITICS

ROOTS OF CONTEMPORARY ISSUES

Series Editors

Jesse Spohnholz and Clif Stratton

The **Roots of Contemporary Issues** Series is built on the premise that students will be better at facing current and future challenges, no matter their major or career path, if they are capable of addressing controversial issues in mature, reasoned ways using evidence, critical thinking, and clear written and oral communication skills. To help students achieve these goals, each title in the Series argues that we need an understanding of the ways in which humans have been interconnected with places around the world for decades and even centuries.

Published

Ruptured Lives: Refugee Crises in Historical Perspective
Jesse Spohnholz, Washington State University

Power Politics: Carbon Energy in Historical Perspective
Clif Stratton, Washington State University

Chronic Disparities: Public Health in Historical Perspective
Sean Wempe, California State University, Bakersfield

Forthcoming

Heavy Traffic: The Global Drug Trade in Historical Perspective
Ken Faunce, Washington State University

Gender Rules: Identity and Empire in Historical Perspective
Karen Phoenix, Washington State University

Power Politics

Carbon Energy in Historical Perspective

Roots of Contemporary Issues

Clif Stratton

Washington State University

New York   Oxford
OXFORD UNIVERSITY PRESS

Oxford University Press is a department of the University of Oxford.
It furthers the University's objective of excellence in research, scholarship,
and education by publishing worldwide. Oxford is a registered trade mark of
Oxford University Press in the UK and certain other countries.

Published in the United States of America by Oxford University Press
198 Madison Avenue, New York, NY 10016, United States of America.

© 2021 by Oxford University Press

Library of Congress Cataloging-in-Publication Data
Names: Stratton, Clif, 1980- author.
Title: Power politics : carbon energy in historical perspective / Clif
    Stratton, Washington State University.
Description: New York : Oxford University Press, [2021] | Series: The roots
    of contemporary issues | Includes bibliographical references and index.
    | Summary: "A higher education history textbook that focuses on carbon
    energy in world history. This is part of the Roots of Contemporary
    Issues series"—Provided by publisher.
Identifiers: LCCN 2020008900 (print) | LCCN 2020008901 (ebook) | ISBN
    9780190696221 (paperback) | ISBN 9780197520581 | ISBN 9780197535325
    (epub) | ISBN 9780190696276
Subjects: LCSH: Energy consumption—History. | Fossil fuels—Political
    aspects—History. | Energy development—Political aspects—History. |
    Energy industries—Political aspects—History. | Energy policy—History.
    | World politics.
Classification: LCC HD9502.A2 S796 2021 (print) | LCC HD9502.A2 (ebook) |
    DDC 333.8/209—dc23
LC record available at https://lccn.loc.gov/2020008900
LC ebook record available at https://lccn.loc.gov/2020008901

Printing number: 9 8 7 6 5 4 3 2 1
Printed by LSC Communications, Inc., United States of America

CONTENTS

LIST OF MAPS AND FIGURES

Maps

Figures

ABOUT THE AUTHOR

Clif Stratton teaches history at Washington State University and serves as the Director of University Common Requirements, WSU's general education curriculum. He is the author of *Education for Empire: American Schools, Race, and the Paths of Good Citizenship* (University of California Press, 2016). A co-designer of the Roots of Contemporary Issues course at WSU, Stratton is the recipient of numerous teaching awards, including the Eugene Asher Teaching Award from the American Historical Association and the President's Distinguished Teaching Award from Washington State University.

ACKNOWLEDGMENTS

Often the preparation of a book about history involves long stretches of solitude spent poring over sources, scholarship, and one's own narrative. Thankfully, the experience of writing this book was not like that. It began in 2014 as a new lesson plan that I foisted upon a lively bunch of unsuspecting first-year students in my Roots of Contemporary Issues course at Washington State University. It was rough, comprised of a set of case study readings, classroom discussions, and lectures about how carbon energy and politics have intersected over time. Those early students and those who came along later and read early draft chapters took it in stride. They raised critical questions and were not scared to admit confusion and offer useful suggestions. And best of all, they discovered all sorts of connections between the history discussed therein and contemporary developments. These hundreds of students have shaped this project from the beginning. I owe each of them a debt of gratitude.

When the project became part of a potential new series in 2016, I became part of a writing team with Ken Faunce, Karen Phoenix, Jesse Spohnholz, and Sean Wempe. I found this process, which involved regular comment on each other's drafts, to be of utmost help in structuring the narrative, framing research questions, simplifying prose, and making the outcome more accessible and clearer than earlier versions. I thank each of them immensely for their critical eyes, encouragement, and collegiality. It has been an absolute pleasure to share this project with them. I especially thank Jesse Spohnholz for being such a wonderful friend, colleague, and series co-editor.

I am also grateful for the influence and guidance, both direct and indirect, of many other academic friends and colleagues on this project, including Isa Blumi, Casey Cater, Kaja Cook, Julian Dodson, Lawrence Hatter, Jeff Sanders, Heather Salter, and Katy Whalen. The wide-ranging influence of scholars of energy, colonialism, capitalism, and global politics warrants acknowledgment too. I have tried to provide such recognition in the references and further readings sections. Of course, any errors in fact or interpretation are my own.

At Oxford University Press, I thank Katie Tunkavige, Patricia Berube, Danica Donovan, and Simone Rico, and others unknown to me for making the production process a breeze. I especially thank Charles Cavaliere, our fearless editor, who took a chance on this series. His patience and direction are unparalleled.

As always, special thanks to Kristen for her enduring love and encouragement. And to our wonderful children Inman, Livie, and Lane: I hope that this book contributes in some small way to a better, more sustainable world as you each grow into adults.

Connecting the Past and Present

Let's begin with events taking place in the last few years. Here's one: in early 2019, Starbucks announced plans to replace plastic straws with recyclable polypropylene lids. "Starbucks is finally drawing a line in the sand and creating a mold for other brands to follow," stated the company's director of packaging. Some supporters see the move as a good example of a market-based solution to environmental damage. Critics warn that it's unlikely that many "green" lids will end up at recycling facilities, since the plan is only slated for stores in two of the seventy-six countries where the company operates, the United States and Canada, which recycle very few polypropylene plastics. Most people agree, though, that plastic pollution has become a problem; worldwide production of plastics in the last few generations has skyrocketed. Many plastics produced today only ever get used for just a few minutes or hours, and then are left for centuries to pollute the earth. Plastics float in enormous masses in our oceans, killing birds, fish, seals, whales, and turtles. They break down into microplastics, making their way into all kinds of organisms. Microplastics found in drinking water are even changing humans' body chemistry. Whose responsibility it is to solve this problem? What solutions are likely to be effective? We will be in a better position to answer those questions if we stop to understand the economic, cultural, political, and social forces that allowed such widespread global plastic pollution to develop in the first place.

Here's another example: On January 28, 2019 the rapper 21 Savage sung a lyric on NBC's *Late Night with Jimmy Fallon* criticizing the US government's policy of separating children from parents who had arrived at the US-Mexico border seeking asylum. A few days later, the US Immigration and Customs Enforcement (ICE) arrested 21 Savage, just a week before the Grammy Awards, for which he had been nominated for his recent collaboration with Post Malone. It turns out the Atlanta-based musician had been brought to the US as a minor by his parents, who failed to renew his visa when it expired. During the Grammys, 21 Savage sat in an ICE detention facility. Supporters of 21 Savage applaud his bringing attention to what they consider an inhumane US immigration policy. Those who disagree with him emphasize the importance of protecting the integrity of national borders and prosecuting violations of American immigration laws. 21 Savage's case became part of a nationwide debate in the US about the arrival of asylum seekers fleeing gang violence in El Salvador, Guatemala, and Honduras, and the US's government's policy of incarcerating children and separating them from their parents. Disagreements on this issue have overlapped with discussions about asylum seekers from the Syrian Civil War as well as about migrants from Latin America who come to the US to work, mostly in the agricultural and service industries, but do not get visas or overstay their visas. But questions about immigration policy and how to response to asylum seekers are by no means limited to the US. In the last couple of years, politicians and ordinary people have been debating similar questions about immigration driven by persecution, poverty, fear of violence, and other hardships in countries such as Lebanon, Turkey, Germany, Britain, India, Bangladesh, Colombia, Brazil, Kenya, and Ethiopia. But too often political dialogue on these issues feels like everyone's goal is to convince others that they are wrong, and treat changing one's mind as a failure rather than as a success. As with the example of plastic, if we work to understand the historical factors that led to these situations, we'll be far better poised to solve problems effectively, instead of contributing to increased polarization.

Here's a third example: a man who murdered over fifty Muslim worshippers in Christchurch, New Zealand in March 2019 was found to have been sharing white nationalist ideas with likeminded people on Facebook and Instagram in the runup to his attack. It turns out that a man who murdered nine African Americans worshipping in a church in Charleston, South Carolina four years earlier had also been using Facebook to exchange hateful and racist ideas with others. Certainly, social media has given people a new platform to spew hate speech, but is there really a relationship between increased racist violence and our new forms of digital communication? After the Christchurch killings, Facebook's executives decided that there was. They announced that the company would remove all white nationalist content from posts on Facebook and its subsidiary, Instagram. Supporters cheered that this massive social media company was taking responsibility to limit hate speech. Critics warned against limiting free speech online. Debate has also centered on whether private companies or governments should be responsible for regulating hate speech and/or protecting free speech. Meanwhile, others worry that extremists are only migrating to new venues, including to the dark web, where they can plot violence free of any oversight. At times one might feel paralyzed by the situation. We want to limit mass violence, but should we accept restrictions on our freedoms to do so? There are other important questions connected to this one. Should anyone be responsible for governing speech on social media? If so, who? And how should do they it? How else could we respond to incidents of mass violence? Often discussions on these topics are guided by people earning ad revenues for every click offering easy-to-understand and/or frantically delivered messages. Fortunately, understanding the longer history of topics like censorship, racism, communication revolutions, and mass violence allows us to take a broader, more mature perspective. Rather than feeling paralyzed, studying the past allows us to make informed decisions about issues and leaves us empowered to help shape the future.

One last example. As the first volumes of this book series entered production in early 2020, a novel coronavirus, which causes the sometimes fatal respiratory illness known as COVID-19, was spreading rapidly throughout the world. First detected in Wuhan, China in late 2019, coronavirus spread to 183 countries and territories in a matter of months. By early April 2020, more than 73,000 people had died, with more than 1.3 million confirmed infections.

In response to this pandemic, national governments have taken uneven measures. South Korea aggressively tested, tracked, and treated in order to slow the spread of the disease. British Prime Minister Boris Johnson faced criticism for his government's more meager response. Johnson delayed the closure of schools, bars, restaurants, museums, and other common gathering spots, even as positive cases in the United Kingdom surpassed 1,300 in mid-March. By early April, Johnson himself landed in intensive care with COVID-19 symptoms.

While we do not yet know the long-term outcomes of the coronavirus pandemic, it has already begun to expose the degree to which the rapid circulation of goods and people throughout the world exposes us all to health threats, even if it does so unevenly. This novel coronavirus has revealed deep global inequities in access to medical care, adequate nutrition, and stable employment that make one more or less likely to contract and survive disease. It has left many societies caught up in a web of just-in-time supply chains woefully underprepared to combat the health threat. The pandemic has exposed the dangers of rapid global travel in spreading disease and highlighted humans' reliance on that same global transportation to share medical supplies and health care personnel. Many advocates of open borders around the world, for example, are supporting border closures to slow the spread of the disease. At least in April 2020, many politicians in the United States seem to be rapidly shifting their positions on policies related to incarceration, debt collection, health care, and guaranteed basic income. The pandemic has also raised important questions about the threats to public health from the intentional and unintentional spread of disinformation. In short order, coronavirus has made us all comprehend just how dependent we are on our fellow humans, for better and for worse. Coronavirus did not create the problems that it has exposed. A purely medical response to the disease will not solve those problems either. But understanding the historical origins of intertwined economic, political, and social developments that shape its spread will put all of us in a better position to address current and future problems rendered acute by disease.

It is the premise of this book series that addressing the aforementioned issues and others facing us today requires understanding their deep and global historical roots. Today's problems are not simply the outcomes of decisions yesterday—they are shaped by years, decades, and centuries of historical developments. A deep historical understanding helps us understand the present-day world in more sophisticated, mature, and reasoned ways. Humans have been interconnected with faraway places for centuries; solving the central problems facing our world means understanding those connections over time.

Too often our popular political dialogue—increasingly driven by social media, partisan politics, and short-term economic interests—ignores or discounts the complex historical dimensions of current issues and thus fails to provide useful contexts for those issues that could help citizens and leaders resolve them. Historians can help their fellow citizens make decisions by explaining the historical developments that created the world we inherited.

Rather than survey all of world history, each book in this series begins in the present with a pressing or seemingly intractable problem facing humanity (i.e., climate change, terrorism, racism, poverty). It then helps us better understand that not only is that problem not intractable but it has historical origins. That is, it has not been a problem since time immemorial, nor is it unique to the present. Rather, problems have historical lives, have undergone changes both subtle and dramatic, and are the outcomes of human decisions and actions. The book in front of you and others in this series will help you: (1) understand the deep historical roots of a pressing and controversial issue facing the world today; (2) understand its global context; (3) interpret evidence to make reasoned, mature conclusions; (4) evaluate the arguments of others surrounding those issues; and (5) identify and utilize research skills to make independent conclusions about contemporary issues of interest to you.

The Case for the Roots of Contemporary Issues

Five central arguments shape this series' scope. First, every book explains why history matters now. Widespread consensus abounds that history helps individuals make reasonable decisions about the present and future. This is why so many governments require that their citizens study history. And yet, in the United States at least, history is pretty consistently among the least popular subjects for high school and college students. Why is this? The answer is probably in part because it is required and because we give so much attention in our society to prioritizing personal and short-term interests, such that studying history seems impractical. Books in this series are explicit about how essential, practical, and empowering studying history is.

Second, all books in the series offer world history, rather than histories of "civilizations" or continents. None of these books, for instance, stops at the history of the "West." There is a good reason for this: the very idea of the "West" only emerged as an effort to imagine a fundamental civilizational distinctiveness that has never existed. The "West" developed in response to interactions between people in Europe and North America with peoples around the world. The "West" offered a politically motivated myth of a linear inheritance from Greece and Rome to modern Europe, and from modern Europe to the United States. But many facts had to be omitted (intentionally or unintentionally) to sustain that argument.

The idea of the "West" had its core in some kind of definition of Europe, and tacked on the majority-white populations in settler colonies in North America, Australia, and elsewhere. That is, the definition of the "West" is rooted in ideas about race and in global racism, which were not just products of internal developments (i.e., developments taking place exclusively within Europe and the United States), but also of the centuries-long interactions of people around the globe, including systems of colonialism and slavery. In short, these volumes recognize that humans have interacted across large spaces for centuries, and that many of the geographical terms that we use to understand the world—the West, Middle East, the Far East, Europe, America, Africa—only came to exist as products of those interactions.

Third, while all volumes in the series offer world histories, they are also different from most world histories in that they focus on the history of a specific issue. In our view, a central challenge facing a lot of world history is the magnitude of coverage required by adopting a global scope. Some solve this problem by dividing up the world into continents. That approach can be effective, but suffers from the same challenge as books that adopt civilizational paradigms like "the West." Others attempt to solve the problem by adopting global narratives that replace older civilizational ones. Global approaches can help us see patterns previously overlooked, but risk erasing the complexity of human experiences and decisions in order to tell universalizing stories that can make the outcomes look inevitable. They often do not capture the extent to which even major outcomes—political revolutions, technological changes, economic transformations—are the products of decisions made by ordinary people. Neither can they capture the logical counterpoint: that those people could have made other decisions, and that ordinary people actually do transform the world every day.

The fourth argument that shapes the scope of this series relates to the interconnection between premodern and modern history. What does "modern" signify in the first place? Most understandings of the past rely on this concept, but its meaning is notoriously hard to pin down. One easy way to think about the options is to look at how historians have divided up history into premodern and modern eras in textbooks and classes.

One common dividing point is 1500. The argument here is that a set of shifts between roughly 1450 and 1550 fundamentally transformed the world so that the periods before and after this period can be understood as distinct from one another. These include global explorations, the information revolution associated with the invention of the printing press, a set of military campaigns that established the boundaries of lands ruled by Muslim and Christian princes, and the spread of Renaissance capitalism.

Another common dividing point between the modern and premodern is 1800. Critical here are the development of industrial production and transportation, democratic forms of governance, waves of anticolonial revolutions in the Americas, novel forms of Western imperialism that came to dominate much of Africa and Asia, the intensification of scientific understandings of the world, and the spread of new secular ideologies, like nationalism. There are other dividing points that historians have used to separate history, but these two are the most common.

Regardless of which breaking point you find most convincing, there are at least two problems with this way of dividing histories along "modern" and "premodern" lines. First, these divisions are usually Eurocentric in orientation. They presuppose that "modernity" was invented in Europe, and then exported elsewhere. As a result, peoples whose histories are divided up differently or that are less marked by European norms wrongly appear "backward." The second problem with these divisions is that they are less capable of identifying continuities across these divides.

We are not arguing that distinguishing between "modern" and "premodern" is always problematic. Rather, we see advantages to framing histories *across* these divides. Histories that only cover the modern period sometimes simplify the premodern world or treat people who lived long ago as irrelevant, often missing important early legacies. Meanwhile, histories that only cover premodern periods often suffer because their relevance for understanding the present is hard to see. They sometimes ask questions of interest to only professional historians with specialized knowledge. This series seeks to correct for each of these problems by looking for premodern inheritances in the modern world.

The final argument that shapes the series is that we have a stronger understanding of developments when we study the interrelationships among large structures of power, processes of change, and individual responses to both. The books work to help you understand how history has unfolded by examining the past from these three interactive perspectives. The first is structural: how political, economic, social, and cultural power functioned at specific times and places. The second explains what forces have led to transformations from one condition to another. The third looks at how individuals have responded to both structures and changes, including how they resisted structures of power in ways that promoted change.

Historians distinguish between structure, change, and agency. Leaving out agency can make structures and changes look inevitable. Leaving out change flattens out the world, as if it were always the same (hint: always be skeptical of a sentence that begins with: "Throughout history"!). Leaving out structures celebrates human choices and autonomy, but naively ignores how broader contexts limit or shape our options. Understanding how structure, change, and agency interact allows us to create a more realistic picture of how the world works.

Doing History

When we talk to authors about writing these books, we urge that they do not need to provide all the answers to the issues about which they write, but should instead provide readers with the skills to find answers for themselves. That is, using the goals just described, this series is meant to help you think more critically about the relationship between the past and the present by developing discrete but mutually reinforcing research and analytical skills.

First, the volumes in this series will help you learn how to ask critical historical questions about contemporary issues—questions that do not beg simplistic answers but instead probe more deeply into the past, bridge seemingly disconnected geographies, and recognize the variety of human experiences. Second, you will learn how to assess, integrate, and weigh against each other the arguments of scholars who study both historical and contemporary issues. Historians do not always agree about cause and effect, the relative importance of certain contributing factors over others, or even how best to interpret a single document. This series will help you understand the importance of these debates and to find your own voice within them.

Third, you will learn how to identify, evaluate, interpret, and organize varieties of primary sources—evidence that comes from the periods you are studying—related to specific historical processes. Primary sources are the raw evidence contained in the historical record, produced at the time of an event or process either by a person or group of people directly involved or by a first-hand observer. Primary sources nearly always require historians to analyze and present their larger significance. As such, you will learn how to develop appropriate historical contexts within which to situate primary sources.

While we listed these three sets of skills in order, in fact you might begin with any one of them. For example, you may already have a historical question in mind after reading several recent news articles about a contemporary problem. That question would allow you to begin searching for appropriate debates about the historical origins of that problem or to seek out primary sources for analysis. Conversely, you might begin searching for primary sources on a topic of interest to you and then use those primary sources to frame your question. Likewise, you may start with an understanding of two opposing viewpoints about the historical origins of the problem and then conduct your own investigation into the evidence to determine which viewpoint ultimately holds up.

But only after you have developed each of these skills will you be in a position to practice a fourth critical skill: producing analytical arguments backed by historical evidence and situated within appropriate scholarly debates and historical contexts. Posing such arguments will allow you to make reasoned, mature conclusions about how history helps us all address societal problems with that same reason and maturity. We have asked authors to model and at times talk through these skills as they pertain to the issue they have contributed to the series.

Series Organization

Each volume in this series falls under one of five primary themes in history. None attempt to offer a comprehensive treatment of all facets of a theme but instead will expose you to more specific and focused histories and questions clearly relevant to understanding the past's impact on the present.

The first theme—Humans and the Environment—investigates how we have interacted with the natural world over time. It considers how the environment shapes human life, but also how humans have impacted the environment by examining economic, social, cultural, and political developments. The second theme, Globalization, allows us to put our relationship to the natural world into a greater sense of motion. It explores the transformations that have occurred as human relationships have developed across vast distances over centuries. The third theme, the Roots of Inequality, explores the great disparities (the "haves" and "have-nots") of the world around us, along lines of race, gender, class, or other differences. This approach allows us to ask questions about the origins of inequality, and how the inequalities in the world today relate to earlier eras, including the past five hundred years of globalization.

Diverse Ways of Thinking, the fourth theme, helps us understand the past's diverse peoples on their own terms and to get a sense of how they understood one another and the world around them. It addresses the historical nature of ideologies and worldviews that people have developed to conceptualize the differences and inequalities addressed in the inequality theme. The fifth theme, the Roots of Contemporary Conflicts, explores the historical roots of conflicts rooted in diverse worldviews, environmental change, inequalities, and global interactions over time. Its goal is to illuminate the global and local factors that help explain specific conflicts. It often integrates elements of the previous four themes within a set of case studies rooted in the past but also helps explain the dramatic changes we experience and/or witness in the present.

Our thematic organization is meant to provide coherence and structure to a series intended to keep up with global developments in the present as historians work to provide essential contexts for making sense of those developments. Every subject facing the world today—from responding to COVID-19 to debates about the death penalty, from transgender rights to coal production, and from the Boko Haram rebellion in Nigeria to micro-aggressions in Massachusetts—can be better understood by considering the topic in the context of world history.

History is not a path toward easy solutions: we cannot simply copy the recommendations of Mohandas Gandhi, Sojourner Truth, Karl Marx, Ibn Rushd, or anyone else for that matter, to solve problems today. To do so would be foolhardy. But we can better understand the complex nature of the problems we face so that the solutions we develop are mature, responsible, thoughtful, and informed. In the following book, we have asked one historian with specialized knowledge and training in this approach to guide you through this process for one specific urgent issue facing the world.

—Jesse Spohnholz and Clif Stratton

ROOTS OF CONTEMPORARY ISSUES

POWER POLITICS

INTRODUCTION

Climate Politics

The famed "window of opportunity" for abolishing the fossil economy and stabilising climate within tolerable bounds—even returning it to safer conditions—is still there; if emissions were reduced to zero the rise in temperatures would soon taper off. Such an enterprise would have to stage a full-scale onslaught on the structural nightmares bequeathed by the past. It would be a revolution against history, an exodus, an escape from it in the last moment, and it would have to know what it has to struggle against.[1]

—ANDREAS MALM, *Fossil Capital, 2016*

In a March 2017 interview, Scott Pruitt, the recently appointed Administrator of the United States Environmental Protection Agency (EPA), called into question the global scientific consensus about human-induced climate change. "I think that measuring with precision human activity on the climate is something very challenging to do and there's tremendous disagreement about the degree of impact, so no, I would not agree that it's a primary contributor to the global warming that we see," Pruitt claimed.[2]

Pruitt directly contradicted the EPA's own website and the United Nations Intergovernmental Panel on Climate Change (IPCC), the leading global organization that makes climate policy recommendations based on scientific data. In its Fifth Assessment Synthesis Report, the IPCC argued: "Human influence on the climate system is clear, and recent anthropogenic emissions of greenhouse gases are the highest in history . . . Warming of the climate system is unequivocal, and since the 1950s, many of the observed changes are unprecedented." The report served as the scientific basis for the 2015 Paris Climate Agreement in which almost two

---

1. Andreas Malm, *Fossil Capital: The Rise of Steam Power and the Roots of Global Warming* (New York: Verso, 2016), 10.

2. Quoted in Chris Mooney and Brady Dennis, "On Climate Change, Scott Pruitt Causes an Uproar—and Contradicts the EPA's Own Website," *Washington Post*, March 9, 2017, https://www.washingtonpost.com/news/energy-environment/wp/2017/03/09/on-climate-change-scott-pruitt-contradicts-the-epas-own-website/?utm_term=.231d10967570.

hundred national governments, along with the European Union, committed to carbon emissions reductions.[3]

But the Paris Climate Agreement has only proven as effective as the sincerity of its signatories. In May 2017, US President Donald Trump announced the United States' withdrawal, citing his position as the elected representative of "the citizens of Pittsburgh, not Paris." In retort, Pittsburgh's mayor reminded Trump that Pittsburgh had voted for his Democratic challenger in the 2016 election and that the city would become 100 percent dependent on renewable energy by 2035.[4] In this exchange, climate change and the carbon energy sources that cause it could not have been more political.

Pruitt, who resigned from the EPA in July 2018 amidst multiple ethics scandals, and his successor, former coal industry lobbyist Andrew Wheeler, deny human activity contributes significantly or at all to climate change. In early 2019, Wheeler denied his denialism in his Senate confirmation hearings, but still considered the climate change threat relatively minor. In usual hyperbolic fashion, Trump has infamously called climate change a "Chinese hoax" on the assumption that the United States' main economic rival is simply suckering Americans into reducing their carbon output to the peril of US economic power. Like many of his predecessors, he has repeatedly advocated continued exponential consumption of coal, oil, and natural gas—the carbon-based fuels that create the greenhouse gases responsible for atmospheric warming. The administration's position is markedly different than other leading approaches to climate change.

The Climate Leadership Council (CLC), a conservative policy group based in Washington, DC and London, argues that for too long conservatives have denied the risks of inaction on climate change. Instead, CLC urges conservatives to promote solutions to a very real global environmental crisis that advance conservative economic and political ideas. According to CLC, "Any climate solution should be based on sound economic analysis and embody the principles of free markets and limited government."[5]

---

3. Intergovernmental Panel on Climate Change, *Climate Change 2014 Synthesis Report Summary for Policymakers*, accessed May 25, 2017, http://ar5-syr.ipcc.ch/ipcc/ipcc/resources/pdf/IPCC_SynthesisReport.pdf.

4. Abigail Abrams, "Pittsburgh Mayor Bill Peduto Hits Back at President Trump: 'We Will Follow the Guidelines of the Paris Agreement,'" *Time*, June 1, 2017, http://time.com/4802340/paris-agreement-pittsburgh-mayor-bill-peduto-donald-trump/.

5. James A. Baker III, Martin Feldstein, Tad Halstead, N. Gregory Mankiw, Henry M. Paulson Jr., George P. Shultz, Thomas Stephenson, and Rob Walton, "The Conservative Case for Carbon Dividends: How a New Climate Strategy Can Strengthen Our Economy, Reduce Regulation, Help Working-Class Americans, Shrink Government, and Promote National Security," Climate Leadership Council, accessed May 18, 2017, https://www.clcouncil.org/wp-content/uploads/2017/02/TheConservativeCaseforCarbonDividends.pdf.

CLC's position on climate change, while a stark departure from climate denialism of the Trump administration, remains largely within the basic ideological framework of market capitalism to which Pruitt and Wheeler also subscribe. The logic goes that if markets functioned in ways that incentivize reductions in carbon energy use, then consumers would take rational, self-interested steps to reduce consumption. Where those incentives will come from remains a crucial question. As critic Kate Aronoff commented, "If the private sector was set up to take on the climate crisis, it probably would have already."[6]

Climate change has also galvanized elements of the political Left. Journalist Naomi Klein has argued that "We have not done the things that are necessary to lower emissions because those things fundamentally conflict with deregulated capitalism, the reigning ideology for the entire period [in which] we have been struggling to find a way out of this crisis." Klein posits that deregulated capitalism "was always about using . . . sweeping [trade] deals . . . to lock in a global policy framework that provided maximum freedom to multinational corporations to produce their goods as cheaply as possible and sell them with as few regulations as possible—while paying as few taxes as possible." Climate change, she asserts, is the most threatening environmental consequence of that policy framework.[7]

As you have probably gathered by now, the CLC and Klein both agree that climate change is real, though they likely disagree about its urgency. But they unequivocally disagree about how to solve it. While the CLC advocates deploying free market principles, Klein calls for eviscerating those free market principles entirely. Indeed, as CLC founder Ted Halstead told National Public Radio in 2017, "I think that in the politics of climate change, the blame can be shared . . . If you listen to the celebrity authors within the green Left . . . like Naomi Klein . . . she actually suggests de-growth and blowing up the economic system. When Republicans hear things like that, it is so fundamentally at odds with their worldview, of course they are going to be tempted to question the science."[8]

Given the overwhelming scientific consensus that human consumption of coal, oil, and natural gas has raised global temperature at heretofore unprecedented rates, why is climate change so divisive? Once a scientific consensus that burning carbon fuels contributes to global warming emerged in the early 1990s (and as it

6. Jon Wiener, "Kate Aronoff on the Battle of Ideas," January 16, 2019, *Start Making Sense*, coproduced by *The Nation* and the *LA Review of Books*, podcast, 37:55, https://audioboom .com/posts/7145443-the-anti-immigrant-temptation-on-the-left-david-adler-on-politics-pedro-noguera-on-the-la-teach.

7. Naomi Klein, *This Changes Everything: Capitalism vs. the Climate* (New York: Simon & Schuster, 2014), 18–19.

8. "Conservatives Make the Case for Action on Climate Change," the1a.org, February 16, 2017, http://the1a.org/shows/2017-02-16/conservatives-make-the-case-for-action-on-climate-change.

turns out among Exxon scientists in the 1970s), why have the world's governments so far been unable to make serious headway in avoiding the most disastrous impacts of climate change?

The central premise of this book is that in order to generate real solutions to the problem of climate change, we must first understand how our relationship to the carbon-based fuels that drive global warming has unfolded over time. Addressing the monumental problem of climate change requires an investigation into the historical exercise of power by carbon energy companies, government officials, and ordinary citizens and workers. It means understanding how and why fossil fuels became inextricably linked to the larger processes and systems of colonization, capitalism, industrial production, consumption, war-making, diplomacy, and others.

By tracing the historical relationship between carbon energy and political ideas, institutions, motivations, and actions, we will be in a better position to understand the entrenched nature of climate change denialism, capitalists' self-proclaimed ability to correct the problem, and the appeal of politically radical solutions to global warming. We need not only understand the scientific underpinnings of global warming—which I will leave to the climate scientists—but equally so the political history of the carbon age that has given rise to the crisis at hand. Climate change requires science to understand it, but addressing it effectively requires political solutions rooted in a historical analysis of the problem.

Politics pervades this book. It's in the title. But before we begin exploring its relationship to carbon energy, I want to be clear about what I do and do not mean by *politics*. I do not mean merely formal acts or spaces of political engagement: campaigns, elections, voting booths, or legislative chambers. This understanding of politics is—while important—too narrow for understanding the wide array of historical participants during the carbon age.

Many of those producing or consuming fossil fuels or the objects those fuels helped create had little or no access to these political spaces. Enslaved Africans who grew sugar in the Caribbean for export to England, where an increasing mass of laborers turned those calories into energy for coal-fired factory work, had no formal political rights. Their compatriots in factories—a growing number of whom were women—had few or no formal political rights either.

But their very existence within the economic and social orders of their societies made those populations inherently political. They made claims for improved material circumstances that threatened to reorganize the relations of power: economic, social, and cultural. They became objects of political debate. In short, most aspects of the routine of our lives have political histories and implications. This is what I mean by politics. To suggest otherwise is to foreclose the possibility of critically examining the economic and social forces that shape the world we inhabit.[9]

---

9. Joan Scott, *Gender and the Politics of History* (New York: Columbia University Press, 1999), 9.

Structure

This book is organized into five chapters that move forward in time and offer selected case studies to illustrate how the pursuit of carbon energy and politics intersect and shape each other over time. Roughly speaking, the chapters track five key periods in the political history of carbon energy: the preindustrial, the Industrial Revolution, the ages of empire and mass democracy, the Cold War and decolonization, and the late- and post–Cold War.

Chapter 1 explores the politics of energy before the Industrial Revolution, when people relied almost exclusively on replenished energy, including water and solar-derived plant energy. They did so not because they were environmentalists but because the technologies capable of exploiting fossil fuels en masse did not yet exist.

To be sure, preindustrial production could be as ecologically destructive as industrial methods, but usually on local scales. Case studies in southern Mexico, eastern Africa, and China point to important lessons about how economic activity and political power can threaten social stability through environmental change. The chapter concludes with an examination of why both China and Britain developed *proto-fossil* economies before the Industrial Revolution and how coal came to shape politics and drive social change in each of these societies.

Despite assumptions to the contrary, the Industrial Revolution, the focus of chapter 2, was not inevitable. A whole range of processes and decisions shaped the rise of coal as the prime mover of machines by the mid-nineteenth century. Chapter 2 examines the global, regional, and local preconditions for the first large-scale application of coal-fired steam as a power source for manufacturing in Britain. But even once the technology to exploit coal for mass production was in place, the political will to do so lagged. Water power remained alluring to anyone interested in turning a profit. I leave you—the reader—to find out what really motivated the switch from water to coal.

After Britain's tumultuous "first," the Industrial Revolution went global. As technologies and know-how spread to other parts of Western Europe, North America, and East Asia in the second half of the nineteenth century, industrialization shaped each society that experienced it in unique ways. Case studies in France and Japan highlight the complexity of experiences with this utmost transformative historical process—that of living and working in the carbon age.

Chapter 3 covers the decades spanning 1870 to 1940, which featured two interdependent processes: the rise of mass democracy in the industrializing world on the one hand, and the extension of imperial control throughout much of the nonindustrial world on the other. From Baku to Brussels, Manchester to Mannheim, Paris to Pittsburgh, and in scores of other industrial cities, workers built powerful labor movements to acquire and strengthen collective political rights. The carbon energy that many workers extracted, moved, and put to work in ever larger quantities enabled the rise of what one historian has called "carbon democracy." These workers were not always successful in achieving their goals. But for the first time in history, they possessed critical leverage over the energy sources—coal and oil—without which their societies would grind to a halt.

But as democracy unfolded haltingly and unevenly in the industrializing world, foreign rule visited the world's agricultural societies with wanton destruction. Colonial control followed industrialization in most cases. Hungry for raw materials, agricultural products, labor, and markets, the European powers together with the United States and Japan voraciously carved up much of the rest of the world into colonies, territories, or spheres of influence, thus forcibly bringing those regions into the industrial orbit.

Before 1900, the industrial powers did not usually colonize to capture and control sources of carbon energy, when coal—a rather expensive fuel to transport—was the prime power source. But by the early twentieth century, foreign intervention increasingly featured the search for and control of oil. Chapter 3 concludes with a detailed case study of how the quest to control Mexican oil unfolded during that country's revolution (1911–1920). Mexico highlights, in part, the differences between the political possibilities for industrial societies built on coal versus those built on oil in the first half of the twentieth century. It foretold the relationship between oil production and undemocratic forms of government for much of the rest of the twentieth century.

Chapter 4 explores how carbon energy shaped the early Cold War and placed limits on the success of anticolonial movements after World War II. After Mexico nationalized its oil industry in 1938, the big multinational oil companies based mostly in Britain and the United States sought control over as much of the world's proven oil fields as possible. Oil production became central to what US officials referred to as modernization, an alternative to the more coercive forms of European colonial rule that people in what today we call the Global South fought against at the time.

The Middle East became ground zero for oil politics immediately after World War II. During this early Cold War period, one of the first targets of so-called modernization was Saudi Arabia, where international oil companies partnered with the repressive regime of Ibn Saud in order to secure what was soon to be the largest proven oil reserves outside the Soviet Union. Oil became essential to sustaining and expanding middle-class life in Europe and America and simultaneously served as a political tool to combat the perceived aggressiveness of Soviet communism.

Populations struggling for independence from foreign control were caught in the middle. In Iran, the United States' decision to prop up the British-owned Anglo Iranian Oil Company in the face of nationalization in 1951 reveal the continued dependence of the United States on the political support of its European allies if it was to successfully fend off a Soviet incursion in the region. Similar moves by officials in the foreign-owned Iraq Petroleum Company and their partners in the

British and US governments thwarted attempts at democracy in Iraq in the 1960s and contributed to Saddam Hussein's rise to power. The consequences for Iranians and Iraqis remain profound to this day.

Attempts by Western oil companies to retain full control over Middle East oil proved futile. By the early 1970s, governments in oil-producing countries asserted greater claims over the oil they exported, including higher profits and expanded decision-making power. But big oil had other tricks up its sleeve. Chapter 5 first examines how these international companies created a fake energy crisis in the 1970s. The crisis of 1973–1974 hit oil consumers hard. But it was political in nature and not tied to any real physical energy shortage. And it drove profits through the roof, even as nationalist governments in oil-producing countries demanded and won greater profit sharing for the oil they exported.

The profits derived from the *crisis* allowed the international oil companies to expand their operations into new territories whose populations were often politically and economically vulnerable. The chapter concludes with two case studies in how oil development after formal independence curtailed the prospects for substantive economic and political autonomy. In the Niger River Delta, the Ogoni mounted a valiant but ultimately futile struggle against the collusion between Nigeria's military government and Royal Dutch Shell. Similarly, in the oil fields and along the pipeline routes of the Caucasus Mountain states of Georgia and Azerbaijan, oil production and transport became the cornerstone of post–Soviet capitalism. That politics shared much in common with the past, including shocking levels of violence and surveillance in order to extract and transport carbon energy.

The book concludes with an investigation into grassroots resistance campaigns by indigenous North American communities against the expansion of carbon energy infrastructure as the planet warms. Though wildly diverse in cultural and linguistic backgrounds, these communities share a common historical thread that has proven powerful in the face of environmental disaster: sustained challenges to the global economic order built on carbon energy. Their experiences offer hope for a livable future.

Carbon energy and the quest to harness or curb its power has driven all manner of political choices, movements, and outcomes across the globe over the last quarter millennium and indeed before. The climate crisis demands that we grasp not just the science of the carbon economy but the historical weight of its politics as well.

Choices and Sources

Writing a history of something as complicated as the politics of carbon energy entails making choices. Here, I have tried to offer a historical analysis that balances depth of detail with breadth of coverage. Mexico's early history of oil fascinated me early on in this project, as did Standard Oil's 1948 propaganda film promoting its efforts to develop Saudi Arabian oil. All it took was an intriguing historical account and a rather ridiculous primary source, respectively, for me to develop those case studies further.

Decisions about what to include have also meant less attention to other equally important places and developments in the historical landscape of carbon energy. This volume is meant to equip you with the analytical tools and a model of writing to explore them on your own. For example, Venezuela or Indonesia (critical oil-producing states), or Central Appalachia (US) or Upper Silesia (Poland), where coal production undeniably continues to shape local politics, invite further historical study. Likewise, I urge you explore the historical connections between the battle over Iraqi oil in the 1960s and the 1990 and 2003 US-led invasions of that country. Clearly, the politics of climate science since the 1970s certainly deserves more attention than this modest volume offers. It is my sincere intention that this book inspires new research projects among its readers.

This project, like any other, has also meant making choices about sources and evidence too. To a significant degree, I have relied on the really great work of fellow historians who study carbon energy's political history in more local, national, or regional contexts. You will find their books and articles cited throughout the volume. I am indebted to their thoroughness and expertise. Often when I went into the library stacks to pull a single title, the subject arrangement system meant that I came out with several more books. It proved a wonderful process of discovery in which any researcher can engage.

For primary source materials—the raw evidence of history—I relied on my university's library database subscriptions and more freely available ones like Hathi Trust and Google Books. It involved a lot of trial and error, which only added to the allure of the discovery. I've analyzed primary sources here not to offer a definitive catalog of historical evidence on the subject but instead as a model for you, the reader, to conduct your own investigations into this or a related topic. In short, understanding the politics of carbon energy in historical perspective involves developing and practicing source gathering and analytical skills critical to any research project you might pursue. The investigation will undoubtedly take you beyond prior knowledge and outside your comfort zone. Enjoy the trip.

1
ENERGY AND POLITICS BEFORE THE CARBON AGE

We have been as drops of water,
born in the ocean and sprinkled on the earth
in a gentle rain.
We became a spring,
and then a stream,
and finally a river flowing deeper and stronger,
nourishing all it touches
as it nears its home once again . . .
. . . Sit by a river bank some time
and watch attentively as the river
tells you of your life.

—LAO TZU, *"We Are A River,"* c. sixth century BCE

Recent and otherwise sound and groundbreaking studies have tended to described the Industrial Revolution and its legacies in a few simplistic ways: as a singular event, as the spectacular discovery of the hidden power of fossil fuels, as the sudden availability of those fuels, or some combination of these three. For example, in his 2010 book *Eaarth*, activist Bill McKibben wrote: "If that stable earth allowed human civilization, however, something else created modernity, the world that most of us . . . inhabit. That something was the sudden availability, beginning in the early 18th century, of cheap fossil fuel." In setting up his monumental political history of oil, historian Timothy Mitchell similarly wrote: "Until 200 years ago, the energy need to sustain human existence came almost entirely from renewable sources." Likewise, environmental historians J. R. McNeill and Peter Engelke write matter-of-factly: "Then in late eighteenth-century England the harnessing of coal exploded the constraints of the organic energy regime. With fossil fuels, humankind gained access to eons of frozen sunshine."[1]

What McKibben, Mitchell, McNeill, Engelke, and others intimate here is that the eighteenth century marked a critical turning point in

1. Bill McKibben, *Eaarth: Making a Life on a Tough New Planet* (New York: Times Books, 2010), 27; Timothy Mitchell, *Carbon Democracy: Political Power in the Age of Oil* (London: Verso, 2013), 12; J. R. McNeill and Peter Engelke, *The Great Acceleration: An Environmental History of the Anthropocene since 1945* (Cambridge, MA: Belknap Press, 2014), 8–9.

energy history and ushered in what we could call the "carbon age." In this period, access to coal, oil, and more recently natural gas became essential to nearly all aspects of daily modern life: the production of electricity, transportation, manufacturing, the treatment of disease, and the capacity to make war, leisure, and so on.

It is unlikely that these scholars meant to reduce the Industrial Revolution—defined most simply by the conversion of carbon energy to mechanical power—to a mere discovery or singular occurrence. But to suggest that humans only began to embrace carbon-based fuels in the eighteenth century when Britons developed the necessary technologies to scale up its productive capacity is misleading. To be sure, when James Watt developed in the 1760s a steam engine capable of turning coal's highly concentrated solar energy into reliable mechanical power, coal's importance increased exponentially and eventually went global. But coal, along with oil and natural gas, has a much deeper socioeconomic and political history than both its critics and supporters typically afford it. And all three carbon fuels have even deeper natural histories.

Geologists locate the origins of the carbon fuels we use in abundance today long before the evolution of humans on planet Earth. Between 360 and 290 million years ago, during what one geologist dubbed the Carboniferous period, plant life utterly colonized the Earth's largely low-lying landmasses. This stood in sharp contrast to the Devonian period before it, when most life unfolded beneath the ocean's surface. During the Carboniferous, lush forests sucked up vast amounts of carbon dioxide from the atmosphere and converted the sun's solar power into energy.

For much of the period, forest floors were swampy, muddy, oxygen-deprived bogs that inhibited the natural decay of the massive spongy-celled trees that flourished in such conditions. This was not a linear or singular process, but instead one of constant, if slow, environmental flux and change. After all, the singular landmass known as Pangaea had not yet begun to separate, its components drifting to eventually form the continents recognizable on maps today. Glacial melting and freezing in the Southern Hemisphere caused sea levels to periodically rise and fall. When in retreat, the oceans allowed coastal forests to thrive. When waters once again engulfed those forests, decay slowed or stopped. Where such conditions were present, fallen trees rich in carbon and in the sun's solar energy first transformed into a soggy biomass called peat. Geological heat and pressure then turned peat into hardened, waterless coal.[2] All told, during the Carboniferous, a period comprising just 2 percent of the Earth's history, coal burial rates were 600 times higher than the average for the other 98 percent of the geological record.[3]

---

2. Barbara Freese, *Coal: A Human History* (New York: Penguin, 2003), 17–20.

3. Andreas Malm, *Fossil Capital: The Rise of Steam Power and the Roots of Global Warming* (New York: Verso, 2016), 41.

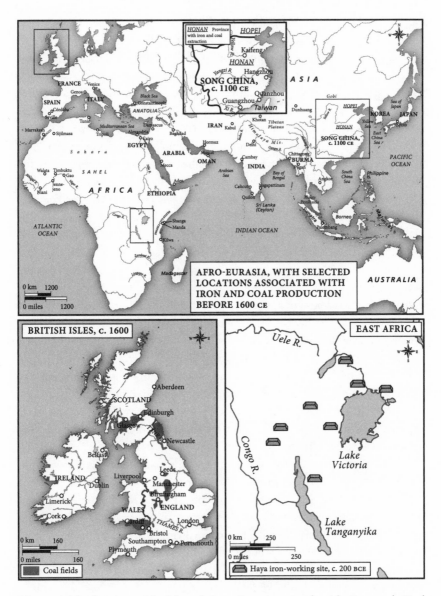

MAP 1.1 Afro-Eurasia, with Selected Locations Associated with Iron and Coal Production Before 1600 CE

Oil and gas, coal's liquid cousins, also began to form during the Carboniferous. As phytoplankton and other organic carbon-heavy plant and animal matter became trapped in sediment deposits at the bottom of oceans, lakes, and later, river deltas, oxygen deprivation turned this matter into kerogen, a polymeric (large chain-like molecule made up of smaller molecules). Geological pressure, heat, and time then caused some kerogens to release their stored carbon molecules as petroleum or natural gas. The process takes on the order of hundreds of thousands of years.[4]

Taken together, the geological origins of coal, oil, and gas make the political struggles to harness that energy seem relatively insignificant within the scope of the Earth's natural history. But the unleashing of that energy, which has begun to alter the Earth's climate in ways that threatens human existence, demands that we understand when, where, and why humans began to rely on carbon energy and further, why that reliance has persisted, even in the face of potential environmental collapse.

At the same time, there is more than a grain of truth to the descriptions of the carbon age offered by the aforementioned scholars. Indeed, in the geological history of Earth, exploitation of carbon energy appears as a blip on the radar. For most of the 3.8 billion of years of terrestrial life, life forms have derived their energy in replenished forms from the sun. Chief among these forms is the energy converted through photosynthesis, whereby plants transform solar energy into digestible forms for humans and other animals. Woody plants that are not readily digestible provide further sources of energy when burned for heat or for the creation of charcoal for manufacturing commodities ranging from iron tools to beer.

If one were to identify the most important human intervention in the Earth's energy regiment, it would most likely not be fossil fuels but the process by which the energy within those fuels and fuelwood is exploited: fire. About half a million years ago our ancestors harnessed this novel form of energy control, and fire was absolutely critical to the first agricultural societies about 10,000 years ago. Because of their relative abundance, accessibility, and renewability, plants—trees in particular—seemed far more efficient sources of heat if burned than something one had to dig out of the ground.

In the roughly 200,000 or so years in which *Homo sapiens* have lived, few populations found coal particularly useful before the last 600 years or so. There are of course important exceptions worth considering. During the Bronze Age, southern Wales' earliest inhabitants used coal for cremation. When the Romans invaded Britain in the first century BCE, they found coal useful not only for ornamental purposes (it could be carved easily) but also because it was combustible. Blacksmiths, soldiers, and priests all burned coal for smelting metal, providing warmth, and honoring Minerva, the goddess of wisdom, respectively.[5]

Sections two and three of this chapter will discuss in greater detail the centrality of coal to iron tool production and other manufacturing activities in imperial

---

4. Jeffrey Dukes, "Burning Buried Sunshine: Human Consumption of Ancient Solar Energy," *Climatic Change* 61, no. 1 (2003): 35–36.

5. Freese, *Coal*, 16–17. W. A. Wrigley describes this preindustrial world of energy as comprised of "organic economies." See Wrigley, *The Path to Sustained Growth* (Cambridge: Cambridge University Press, 2016), 7–18.

China and medieval Britain. But still, by 1800, coal represented only about 10 percent of global commercial energy.[6] In short, the mass exploitation of coal was in no way inevitable in the eighteenth century or before, and neither was oil's by the late nineteenth. A series of human decisions, made within the framework of economic and political structures, created the shift to coal and later oil that transformed the world after 1800.

How then do we situate the exploitation of carbon energy and the politics that governs that exploitation into the whole of human history? Do we stick with the conventional narrative that marks the late eighteenth century as truly unique and representative of dramatic change and ignore what came before as too inconsequential given the changes after the 1760s? Or is it possible to locate the origins or at least examples of carbon politics before the Industrial Revolution? What can we learn in the process of doing so?

This chapter offers three seemingly contradictory arguments about the political history of carbon energy. First, it takes as a central premise that the forms of energy that are so ubiquitous in our lives today—coal, oil, and natural gas—are indeed relatively new features of the world's energy landscape. Thus, we can consider its relationship to forms of political power, labor movements, and environmentalism as something that is new. In this vein, it is in line with much of the best scholarship on the origins and impacts of the Industrial Revolution.

Second, at the same time, carbon energy's importance to politics and to human existence is not as novel as most assume. We should be open to pushing back against common notions of "modern" and "industrial" to identify similarities and parallels between the recent and distant past.

Third, since the distant past featured far more renewable energy than carbon energy, it is important to explore how humans harnessed, controlled, used, and sometimes misused those renewable forms, as well as the limitations they encountered. If we do so, we are likely better able to understand how those who lived long ago bore many of the same daily considerations about energy that we do today, even if that energy came in different forms and people's daily routines looked different than ours.

I am not suggesting that we impose parallels or similarities between the modern and premodern periods that simply do not exist. But if we are to solve the kinds of environmental problems that stem from the use of carbon fuels, we ought to be open to the lessons that the precarbon age can offer. If climate change is the global manifestation of our voracious consumption of carbon fuels, all energy consumption has local impacts on the natural environment as well as on human economics and politics. In that basic sense, our time is not as unique as we think it is.

---

6. Freese, *Coal*, 4–6; Bruce Podobnik, *Global Energy Shifts: Fostering Sustainability in a Turbulent Age* (Philadelphia: Temple University Press, 2006), 18.

Forests

For the moment let us leave aside carbon energy's deeper natural and political histories and examine how replenished sources of energy came to dominate concerns
in a range of societies before 1800. Doing so will allow us to consider both the
changes and continuities in our relationship to nature.

The following examples may seem distant, outdated, and decidedly not modern.
Yet through them we can in fact learn quite a bit about our own political relationship
to the natural world. Each of these societies reached cultural, political, and economic
apexes at certain points in their histories, and then began declines of varied rapidity.
Though by no means the only cause, their collective decisions to use forest resources
in particular ways and with increasing degrees of intensity contributed significantly
to their declines. As we will see, those declines were in no way preordained, and we
ought not to be so arrogant to think that it could not or will not happen to us.

When *Homo sapiens* first emerged 200,000 years ago, the Earth's forests looked
quite different than they do today. Hunter-gatherers that lived during the Pleistocene
developed patterns of consumption and movement in relation to the resources offered by woodlands, which varied in density and biodiversity relative to latitude and
seasonal changes. During the Pleistocene, much more of the Earth's surface was comprised of ice than during the subsequent Holocene. New innovations in hunting and
gathering, including hooks, nets, and stone tools, enabled *Homo sapiens* to deal with
these climatic pressures with greater success than their *Homo habilis* and *Homo erec-
tus* counterparts. Consequently, *Homo sapiens* transformed forests with more regularity and frequency, fished lakes, rivers, and oceans more efficiently, and by the end
of the Pleistocene, had colonized all continents except Antarctica.[7]

The modern forest, which emerged in tandem with agriculture about 10,000
years ago, formed in response to the slow retreat of ice. During the ensuing
Holocene, many plant and animal species quickly adapted to the new climatic
conditions characterized most importantly by temperatures 4 to 5 °C warmer than
the Ice Age. Humans were no exception. "As the forest changed, so humans colonized the newly vegetated land with remarkable rapidity, doing all those things
that humans do: foraging, firing, hunting, selecting species and rejecting others,
turning the soil, fertilizing it, trampling it, and mixing it," as geographer Michael
Williams has noted. All of this activity, which allowed humans to exploit the forest's resources for their survival and expansion, ought not to be seen as a wholly
disruptive intervention in an otherwise undisturbed, steady, cyclical biological process, but rather as an integral part of the forest's evolution.[8]

---

7. Lauren Ristvet, *In the Beginning: World History from Human Evolution to the First States*
(Boston: McGraw Hill, 2007), 16, 23.

8. Michael Williams, *Deforesting the Earth: From Prehistory to Global Crisis* (Chicago:
University of Chicago Press, 2003), 12.

Among the most radical of changes initiated by humans at the outset of the Holocene was the decision to cultivate plants and raise animals rather than forage or hunt for them. This shift was quite uneven. By no means did all humans switch to farming and husbandry, and those that did, often did so only partially at first. And not all settled. But many did, and those decisions necessitated changes in the relationships among each other and with nature.

The need to codify the rules governing a population that was increasing exponentially relative to the land they occupied required the adoption of political structures and practices to which all generally adhered, even if some did so against their will. Further, the decision to stake the bulk of the food supply on relatively few varieties of plants and animals concentrated human energy needs in ways that produced more food but left human settlements open to crop failure, disease, resource depletion, and other biological consequences of dense settlement and farming.[9]

Forests were chief among those natural systems impacted by the agricultural transition after 8,000 BCE. In what is today Europe, denser settlements and more of them demanded evermore fuelwood and construction materials. Humans cultivated certain trees and plants at the expense of others, which led to forest fragmentation. Isolated from the denser mass of woodlands that preceded large-scale human intervention, forests then adopted new biological characteristics. Similar processes unfolded in North America, where the earliest agriculturalists cleared river valley forests to make space for beans, gourds, squash, and fruit- and nut-bearing trees.[10]

Attempts to manage forest resources unfolded in East Africa as well. By 1000 BCE, the Bantu-speaking Haya settled a region then called Buhaya (today, Kagera) along the western shores of Lake Victoria in the modern-day nation-state of Tanzania (see Map 1.1). These settlers, whose ancestors originally migrated from modern-day Cameroon in West Africa, encountered Sudanic speaking peoples already engaged in farming and pastoralism (domestication of animals). The rains that visited the western shores of Lake Victoria made agriculture quite productive, so long as farmers were willing to clear the lakeshore's dense forest.

The Haya organized into small clans based on lineage and readily adopted farming and pastoralism. They fished the lake, traded with their neighbors, and no later than 200 BCE, regularly produced iron. As some Haya clans began to specialize in iron, they gained economic advantages over neighboring groups. Iron clans competed with each other over which could construct the most enduring forges, craft the most effective tuyeres (hand-held blow pipes made of baked clay used to blast air into the forge), and ultimately produce the highest quality iron tools. Winning these competitions granted political and economic advantages in trade with their farming and cattle-herding neighbors.

---

9. For an overview of agriculture's origins and impacts, see Ristvet, *In the Beginning*, 33–73.

10. Williams, *Deforesting the Earth*, 12–13.

With supplies of iron ore in the surrounding hills, iron production expanded, and the tools produced enabled increases in crop yields and consequently increases in population. The expansion of Haya settlements along the lakeshore necessitated forms of centralized political authority, primarily to manage the critical resources that went into the production process: fuelwood, iron ore, and clay.

For a time, this worked well. But by 300 CE, population growth placed untenable strains on woodlands. At the lake's edge, the Haya cleared more land for farming and felled more timber for charcoal to fire iron forges. The resulting erosion degraded soil nutrients. Crop production declined. Archaeological evidence reveals from 300 to 500 CE a steady exodus from the iron villages and the surrounding farmland in favor of western grasslands, which supported cattle grazing. Those that remained at the lakeshore had to venture much further afield to obtain fuelwood. After 600 CE, the once industrious iron forges ceased smelting. The sites were never abandoned completely, as fish, cattle, and some farming allowed smaller numbers of Haya to remain.

Over time, with reduced population pressures, the forests regenerated, and by 1250 CE, population numbers increased again both among the Haya and among recent cattle-herding migrants. Other migrants also brought with them a more varied agricultural portfolio that included bananas. The influx of new crops and cattle manure helped replenish the soil and increased its longevity. Iron production flourished once again. New forge designs and the intermittent use of swamp grasses as fuel rather than timber suggests an increasing concern for forest management.

Nevertheless, by the end of the 1600s, iron production declined again, in part because the cattle-herding clans attempted to assert political control over the lakeshore iron producers and farmers. They withheld manure—a critical soil input—and thus literally used bull shit as political leverage to subordinate neighboring clans. Faced with the prospect of dwindling charcoal resources (swamp grass proved insufficient as fuel), many iron-making clans submitted to the Babito and Bahinda dynasties. The latter took control of the sacred and symbolic iron-producing sites at the lakeshore in order to confer on themselves political legitimacy by forging ties (pun intended) with the region's prosperous iron past. Once they did so, Bahinda rulers organized a central taxation system and direct oversight over iron production.[11]

Like the Haya, the Maya of Mexico's Yucatan peninsula created similar ecological problems that ultimately foiled any intentions of expansion or even political and social stability. By 1000 BCE—around the time the Haya settled the western shores of Lake Victoria—the Maya were industrious agriculturalists and had developed highly sophisticated cultural and political practices. A small number eventually inhabited a ten square mile settlement at Copán in what is today western Honduras. Based on archaeological evidence, the population of Copán likely

11. Peter R. Schmidt, *Iron Technology in East Africa* (Bloomington: Indiana University Press, 1997), 14–21; Ristvet, *In the Beginning*, 53–54.

reached its apex of around 27,000 no later than 900 CE, a fairly average size for most Mayan settlements.

At Copán, Maya grew beans and maize (corn). Maize produced large yields but put extra strain on soil nutrients and the water table. Situated in a river valley surrounded by hills more subject to erosion than the valley below, Copán prospered when most people lived in the valley itself and the hills remained wooded. The forests above the settlement offered the critical function of water cycling in order to ensure steady rainfall in the valley.

As the population grew, Copán's dwellers organized themselves into a hierarchical political structure common among many agricultural societies and already prevalent at other Mayan settlements. Kings and nobles comprised a ruling elite. Kings claimed to divine the necessary inputs for agricultural bounty, especially sufficient and timely rainfall. A large class of agricultural laborers supported the basic energy needs of small numbers of artisans and merchants. But they also provided the labor necessary to maintain the lavish lifestyle of the ruling class. To preserve their authority, kings commissioned the construction of monuments and palaces that stood as symbols of their divinely ordained political authority and if necessary as bulwarks against rebellion from below or rivalry with each other. Nobles followed suit. By 800 CE, there were about 20 such structures, with one exceptional palace comprised of 50 buildings with space to house 250 people.

Equally important to the fate of Copán as the construction and reinforcement of political hierarchy was the increase in the number of people living on the hilled slopes surrounding the river valley. Pollen analysis reveals that clear cutting of trees on the hillsides and hilltops corresponded with the increase in built structures on this elevated terrain and more frequent attempts to grow food high above the riverbed below. Archeological evidence also points to an increased use of hillside trees for fuelwood and for making plaster—the key construction material in the increasingly lavish palaces of the Copán elite. Taken together, settlement and farming by way of clear cutting sent the more acidic hillside soil washing down onto the fertile farmland near the river.

In short order, the little bit of productive farmland that had sustained a modest population of riverbed dwellers now had to support refugees from the hillsides, rapidly depleted of trees and the soil's already marginal nutrients. Infighting for scarce food rations ensued, and malnutrition beset all of Copán (though it was decidedly worse for laborers than for nobles). Given that the king staked his authority on provisions of rain, the man-made drought that deforestation created by interrupting the natural water-cycling process almost certainly threatened his political authority. Studious users of the written word, the Maya at Copán recorded nothing about their king after 822 CE, and in 850 CE, the royal palace burned to the ground.[12]

---

12. Jared Diamond, *Collapse: How Societies Choose to Fail or Succeed* (New York: Penguin, 2005), 157–77.

These examples of the Haya and Maya (and there are many others) ought not to let us slip into thinking about premodern forest users as wholly irresponsible, reckless, or ignorant. They certainly were each of these to some degree, but no more than ourselves, who continue to extract regenerative resources like timber and soil nutrients at rates faster than can be restored through natural processes.

What these examples can instead offer is empathy with those that relied on similar sources of energy as ourselves. They also offer us caution and introspection when we think about whether or not our own political systems are fully equipped to deal with ecological crises and how we might reconfigure those systems in ways that encourage us to use energy more sustainably and equitably.

Hydraulic Politics

So far we have examined how humans have interacted with renewable sources of energy, namely those offered by forests. While forests offered societies ranging in size from a few hundred to hundreds of thousands, the capacity to develop complex social structures, trade networks, political power, manufacturing, and the control of water proved equally important to a smaller number of quite large and powerful empires. In this section, we will explore how political power is contingent not just on renewable sources of energy but also the carbon-based fuels that are the primary subject of this book. For that, we can look to China and its prodigious control of water, as well as its exploitation of coal for the purposes of iron production.

Chinese control of water for commerce, transportation, and agriculture became critical to political power as early as the late third millennium BCE. Indeed, political strength, internal strife, and the inability to fend off outside threats all map rather neatly onto historical patterns of attention and neglect to China's elaborate system of water control. Likewise, China's Song dynasty (r. 960–1279 CE) began to support coal mining in quantities sufficient to power a robust manufacturing sector in the capital city of K'ai-Feng by the eleventh century. But it could only do so with a reliable network of navigable waterways. The Chinese example, in other words, reveals how critical it was to harness two very different kinds of energy in order to sustain political authority in a highly complex and expansive society.

As a hydraulic society, or one that relies primarily on the use of river water for large-scale crop irrigation, water defined much of China's political and economic history, including its founding myth. Numerous imperial government officials, including Han historian Sima Qian (ca. 145–86 BCE), have credited Yu the Great with China's emergence from a loose tribal confederation to a cohesive and ultimately expansive society. It is perhaps no surprise that Yu was a water manager and conservator—a hydraulic engineer, in today's parlance. His ability to organize and channel the unruly floodwaters of the Yellow River prompted tribal leaders to embrace him as an equal, and Yu went on to found the Xia dynasty, which reigned from 2200 to 1750 BCE.

China's founding myth features Yu selflessly diverting excess floodwater from the Yellow River through a series of ditches and canals, including one he bore through a mountain, in order to save the people from the river's destructive forces. Yu's heroics, coupled with his solidarity with ordinary canal workers with whom he labored, endeared him to subsequent rulers. Confucius described Yu as humble, selfless, and highly competent—a model for the technocrats who advised subsequent Chinese emperors.[13]

Following the conquest of the Xia dynasty by the Shang and later Zhou dynasties, water management remained an urgent matter not just for agricultural laborers, but for ruling elites who staked their claims to power on their ability to tame forces of nature. Zhou rulers developed a concept called the Mandate of Heaven. The mandate tied an emperor's political legitimacy not simply to birthright and lineage, but to the divine. The emperor had the approval of the ancestral gods so long as he ensured rain, peace, and bountiful harvests. Droughts, floods, war, and crop failures signified the mandate's revocation, exposed the emperor's moral failure, and opened the door to political challengers.

In retrospect, the mandate was a risky concept on which to stake one's political power. It had the potential for enduring payoffs, but only insofar as the technocrats that served the emperor could successfully do the work of managing China's water resources to prosperous ends.

Water control also framed the famous sixth-century BCE philosophical debates between Taoists and Confucianists over the relationship between humans and the natural world and over the direction of politics. Taoists emphasized the awesome power of water and humans' subordination to it and other forces of nature. State engineers schooled in Taoist teachings designed water control systems that functioned within this philosophical framework. Dams, dikes, and canals channeled rather than impeded the natural flow of rivers. Taoists applied similar logic to politics. They argued that rulers ought to seek legitimacy through moral suasion rather than brute force.

Contrarily, Confucian engineers subscribed to a worldview that largely subordinated nature to man. Confucian waterworks were more obstructive of rivers' natural flows, and perhaps unsurprisingly, their political outlook favored force over persuasion. In the long run, political elites found Confucianism more appealing. In part, this was because it called for the creation and maintenance of a robust and all-powerful bureaucratic apparatus of advisors, resource managers, tax collectors, and military officials that served at the emperor's pleasure. Further, it provided a check against the potential revocation of the Mandate of Heaven should drought or nomadic invasion visit China. This kind of political power, in contrast to the less

---

13. David A. Pietz, *The Yellow River: The Problem of Water in Modern China* (Cambridge, MA: Harvard University Press, 2015), 29–30.

invasive path trod by Taoists, formed the nexus of Chinese imperial power from the Han dynasty (r. 206 BCE–220 CE) through the early twentieth century.[14]

But before the Han came to power, several monumental feats of hydraulic engineering began to turn China into a political, economic, and technological powerhouse. Prior to their ascent to imperial rule over the whole of Chinese lands, the Qin (r. 221–206 BCE) successfully completed the Cheng-kuo Canal in 246 BCE, which diverted water of two Yellow River tributaries to irrigate vast millet-producing fields north of the Qin capital of Xi'an. Three decades before that, Qin rulers appointed a river manager named Li Bing as provincial governor of western Sichuan. Schooled in Taoist principles rather than Confucian ones, Li oversaw the construction of a series of diversion weirs on the Min River, a tributary of the upper Yangtze River. Workers built flexible bamboo cages filled with rocks and situated them in spots where the river's contours enabled diversion of water into inner or outer channels. This allowed workers to redirect water for irrigation or flood control, respectively. The outer channels allowed for the extensive use of waterwheels for hulling rice and powering textile machinery. Centuries later, the Dūjiāngyàn weirs remain in place.

Immediately important, though, is that Li's completion of an irrigation canal to the Chengdu plain brought over 2,000 square miles of land under cultivation. The excess food production helped Qin leaders raise an army of soldiers, engineers, and loyal bureaucrats who helped to consolidate power at the end of what is now called the Warring States period. Once in power, Qin engineers designed and oversaw the construction for the twenty-mile-long Ling Chu, or Magic Canal, the world's first transport canal. Another Taoist-inspired project, the Magic Canal joined northern and southern China at a geographic point where the Xiang River (a Yangtze tributary) and Gui River (a Pearl tributary) flowed in close in proximity to each other.

Once completed, Qin generals could deploy armies as far as the port city of Canton, 1,250 miles south of Xi'an. But as some historians have noted, overcentralization, especially "gigantic projects" like canal and wall building, "strained the empire's resources" and ultimately created the conditions for its downfall. While the Magic Canal allowed Qin rulers to deploy an army of half a million to the south, provisioning that fighting force and administering rule over southern lands proved more difficult. Though relatively short in its distance, the Magic Canal in essence provided the pretext for the failed attempt of the Qin to achieve political unification and the ability of the subsequent Han dynasty to achieve that goal.[15]

---

14. Steven Solomon, *Water: The Epic Struggle for Wealth, Power, and Civilization* (New York: Harper Perennial, 2010), 96–103.

15. Solomon, *Water*, 103–04; Jane Burbank and Frederick Cooper, *Empires in World History: Power and the Politics of Difference* (Princeton, NJ: Princeton University Press, 2010), 48–49.

The Han (r. 206 BCE - 220 CE) centralized nearly all water management and in doing so became the largest landholders. A centralized taxation system and the ability to marshal a vast unpaid labor force enabled Han rulers to maintain, improve upon, and expand the water control systems developed in earlier periods. Industrial production followed, including innovations in iron forging, silk making, and grain hulling. Some of these products, especially silk, became essential items of trade that linked China to the other end of the Eurasian landmass along the later-named Silk Road. Roman elites on the Mediterranean Sea—contemporaries of the Han—clamored for Chinese silk. Silk Road trade enriched the Han state and enabled the extension of trade networks beyond the main east–west overland route to India, Iran, and Southeast Asia.

But Han hegemony remained closely tied to its ability to control rivers. Most surface accounts of the fall of the Han in the early third century CE blame nomadic invaders on China's northern frontier (modern-day Mongolia). While true, those invaders were only able to challenge a weakened Han state, normally defensible by a sizable army in the north. About two centuries before the dynasty's official collapse, river managers were slow to repair hundreds of miles of irrigation and transport canals after epic floods on the Yellow River caused a shift in its course in 11 CE. Food shortages turned into famine, disease, and outmigration. Moreover, the shortages extended to the Han army stationed in the north. Faced with a weakened and undersized defense force, Xiongnu nomad warriors chipped away at Han authority in the region over decades, rendered portions of the Great Wall penetrable and thus ineffective, and gradually brought about the dynasty's demise. Even the customary if tenuous alliances forged through marriages between Han women and Xiongu chiefs could not stave off the political crisis precipitated by water.[16]

On the heels of the Han defeat, China became engulfed in internecine conflict. By the time the Sui consolidated power in 589 CE, many of China's feats of hydraulic construction lay in disrepair. Prodigious builders, the Sui set about the restoration of the empire's key transportation, irrigation, and manufacturing sectors. In addition, 5,000 forced laborers worked at dizzying speed to construct in just six years the 1,100-mile-long imperial Grand Canal that links the Yellow and Yangtze rivers and thus northern and southern China.

The result was "a stupendous 30,000-mile-long national inland waterway system that enabled a united China to ship vital rice supplies grown on the terraced hillside paddies of south China to the large population centers and army troops located on the Yellow River to defend against the continuing threat from bellicose nomadic horsemen from the Asian steppe," as one scholar has described.

16. Solomon, *Water*, 110; Xinru Liu and Lynda Norene Shaffer, *Connections Across Eurasia: Transportation, Communication, and Cultural Exchange on the Silk Roads* (Boston: McGraw Hill, 2007), 30–31.

State granaries and storage facilities situated at strategic locations throughout the system ensured what the Mandate of Heaven dictated: peace and prosperity. Consequently, cultural and technological innovation flourished under the Sui and subsequent T'ang and Song dynasties.[17]

Our goal to this point has not been to stake the entirety of Chinese prosperity or hardship on water management. But surely, without the technical ability and political will to control immense rivers, China would have looked quite different than it did in the third century, the eighth century, or even the twenty-first century. Under successive imperial dynasties, water management generated food abundance, enabled long-distance trade, moved armies, and created taxable markets that enriched the state. Mismanagement tended to coincide with the opposite: famine, economic retraction, and military vulnerability.

Proto-Fossil China

Water also powered industry, and once the Song dynasty (r. 960–1279 CE) ascended to power, iron production quickly eclipsed the capacity of earlier Han iron foundries. Moreover, Song forgers chose to rely increasingly on coal, not fuelwood, as a fuel source. As shown in Map 1.1, the geographic proximity of the Northern Song's urban capital K'ai-Feng to vast stores of iron ore and coal transformed China into the world's first proto-fossil economy.

Though Chinese coal mining existed before the Song dynasty, urban growth in and around K'ai-Feng (see Figure 1.1) facilitated the expansion of iron and coal extraction in the northeastern provinces of Honan and Hopei during the eleventh century. As blacksmiths exhausted timber reserves around several key mines to keep up with demand in K'ai-Feng, they moved their operations closer to the region's coal fields and began to substitute anthracite and bituminous coal for the disappearing sources of charcoal that resulted from deforestation.

The knowledge to do so was already in place. By the fourth century BCE, Chinese smelters had figured out that they could burn anthracite coal in a crucible to make iron. While in power, the Han established forty-eight state iron foundries, which harnessed river power by way of waterwheels to operate the bellows that stoked the furnaces. Charcoal replaced anthracite coal because it burned more efficiently and yielded stronger iron, but by the ninth century CE, smelters had reduced bituminous coal to coke, a hard but porous substance that was cheaper to come by than charcoal. Two centuries later, ironworkers successfully decarbonized iron to make steel. As historian Robert Hartwell notes, "Every single important characteristic of the nineteenth and twentieth century

---

17. Solomon, *Water*, 111–12.

FIGURE 1.1 Kaifeng, view from Longting toward Iron Pagoda (erected 1049 CE), 1910.

native Chinese iron and steel industry had been developed by the end of the eleventh century."[18]

The switch from charcoal to coal in Chinese iron making may have staved off a political crisis that could have brought down the Song dynasty earlier than the Jurchen and later Mongol invasions eventually did in the twelfth and thirteenth centuries, respectively. In 1087, the poet Su Dongpo described coal as the savior that rescued China from an impending ecological crisis brought about by deforestation and that was likely to precipitate a political struggle:

> When, in the year before last, rainstorms and snowfalls had
>   blocked off land-based travel,
> The people of Peng were afflicted—by their shinbones
>   splitting and cracking.
> For half a bundle of sodden firewood they picked up their
>   quilts in their arms

---

18. Robert Hartwell, "A Cycle of Economic Change in Imperial China: Coal and Iron in Northeastern China, 750–1350," *Journal of Economic and Social History of the Orient* 10, no. 1 (June 1967): 118; Solomon, *Water*, 107.

And hammered on doors from dawn till dusk, but nobody
    wanted to barter.
That a rich inheritance lay in their hills was something they
    did not know.
Lovely black rock in abundance, ten thousands of cartloads
    of coal.
No one had noticed the spatters of tar, nor the bitumen,
    where it oozed leaking,
While, puff after puff, the strong-smelling vapors—drifted
    off on their own with the breezes.
Once the leads to the seam were unearthed, it was found to
    be huge and unlimited.
People danced in throngs in their jubilation. Large numbers
    went off to visit it . . .
In the southern hills, rest, and return to life, await the forests
    of chestnuts,
Yet iron, stubborn ore from the hills to the north, will be
    no trouble to smelt.[19]

Su Dongpo described the discovery of coal in the province of Jiangsu, but further west, Honan-Hopei coal had already begun to reinvigorate iron production and manufacturing. By 1078, ironworkers were producing 35,000 tons of pig iron per year, perhaps more than Britain's total output in the early eighteenth century.

We cannot know for sure that coal saved the Song from an uprising from below. But we do know that Song rulers were particularly inclined to tap into the productive capacity of ore and coal mining near K'ai-Feng. The close proximity of coal and iron deposits to the Northern Song capital and to the elaborate system of managed waterways that linked the city to other parts of the empire allowed merchant-entrepreneurs to trade iron products produced with coal for agricultural products like grain. When taxed, a portion of that grain provisioned a robust Song military. And the strong economic foundation created by coal and iron at K'ai-Feng transformed the city into the world's leading manufacturing center. Numerous trade goods, including processed tea, textiles, books, bricks, tiles, porcelain, and much more, flowed from K'ai-Feng throughout the empire and beyond.[20]

Though by no means the only factor, coal and iron made Song China the most formidable political and economic power of the eleventh century. It had become

---

19. Wang Shuizhao, ed., *Su shi xuangji* [An anthology from Su Shi (Dongpo)] (Shanghai: Shanghaiguji chubanshe, 1984), 118, quoted in Mark Elvin, *The Retreat of the Elephants: An Environmental History of China* (New Haven, CT: Yale University Press, 2004), 20–21.

20. Hartwell, "A Cycle of Economic Change in Imperial China," 142–45.

a proto-fossil economy, characterized by regular mining and trade of coal; coal's regular use for heating in homes and industry; and elevated rates of coal consumption, but not so as to stake self-sustaining economic growth on coal itself.[21]

We might expect that through sheer exhaustion of the Honan-Hopei coal and iron reserves, the Song did what many societies in world history have done: deplete resources to the point of either environmental and economic crisis. We have seen how the Maya and Haya pushed the ecological limits in ways that contracted prosperity.

But such an explanation fails to account for the simple fact that as of the 1960s, over 200 million tons of Chinese bituminous coal remained in the ground. Rather, a confluence of factors, each not inevitably destructive on its own, ultimately brought about the abandonment of coal and iron production.

Chief of among these factors was the loss of K'ai-Feng as a regional market for iron products. In the late twelfth century, the Yellow River again shifted course and temporarily severed water transport between the coal and iron fields and the city of K'ai-Feng, where the vast majority of these materials were either consumed or traded elsewhere within and beyond the empire. The Song and subsequent dynasties continued to stake their political power on their ability to control water. An inability to do so meant disruption in nearly all aspects of regional economies impacted by the bursting of dikes or the breakdown of locks.

By the time workers completed the northern extension of the Grand Canal in 1325 and thus reopened K'ai-Feng to trade networks, Chin (Jurchen) and later Yuan (Mongol) economic policy had rendered a comeback for coal and iron unlikely. The Chin doled out land as patronage to noble clans that largely deployed unfree labor for mining and farming. After the likely depopulation of the northern peasantry ahead of rumors of the Mongol invasion, the Yuan replaced patronage with salaried representatives of the government. Their demands more or less fixed in terms of productivity, neither patrons nor government officials had incentive to revive coal and iron production to Song levels, save for the provisioning of the imperial army with iron weapons. Without the necessary incentives, few investors were willing to stake their fortunes in the capital-intensive enterprises of coal and iron production.[22]

We have seen that even in the absence of industrial production on nineteenth-century terms, China was indeed an industrial powerhouse by the eleventh century. Song interest in a robust commercial and industrial economy powered by coal (if not steam) arguably made China the leading political and economic empire of the time. To be sure, it remained vastly ahead of Britain, where industrial producers would not harness buried sunshine on a mass scale until the middle of the

21. Malm, *Fossil Capital*, 52.

22. Hartwell, "Cycles of Economic Change," 148–51, 154.

nineteenth century. But in the meantime, Britons still regarded coal as a critical resource well before James Watt perfected his steam engine.

English Coal

In 731 CE, the English monk St. Bede the Venerable wrote a history of England from the withdrawal of the Romans in the fifth century to his own time. In that eighth-century document, St. Bede described the decline of coal gathering near the River Tyne after the Roman departure, and he noted that if used it all, coal's thick black smoke drove away serpents. The English, in contrast to their Roman occupiers, apparently found little use for coal. But by the eleventh century, as northern China's coal-fired iron production reached its apex, coal once again appeared in England's historical record.

Yet coal's profitability remained quite low because it was too heavy and thus costly to ship long distances, even with access to navigable waterways. And England's tolerance for its noxious odor was thin. Only blacksmiths, masons, and some brewers seemed to use coal as fuel. Many urban dwellers protested the burning of coal. In 1306, for example, Londoners complained to a royal commission about the "infected and corrupted" air caused by coal smoke. The protest led to a temporary ban. However, bigger environmental, political, and economic forces would make coal a hot commodity by 1700. These changes meant that those concerned about health and air quality found fewer royal officials willing to listen.[23]

What changed? Why did the English, who mostly loathed coal in the thirteenth century, begin to embrace it by the end of the sixteenth? Why did coal become the most sought after fuel by 1700? Historians have usually pointed to several somewhat sequential factors that, only taken together, explain the transition. First, following a devastating population decrease at the hands of the bubonic plague in the fourteenth and fifteenth centuries, England's population rebounded. As it did, the forests that had reclaimed much of the farmland left untended faced threats of deforestation. Villagers first razed the woodlands closest to their settlements for fuel, for timber, and to clear pasturage for animals. As they did so, the cost of securing fuel and timber from forests further afield increased precipitously.

Faced with shortages, some moved to larger towns or cities, where the process, also subject to the demands of industry for timber, repeated on a larger scale. As John Nef, arguably the twentieth century's leading historian of the British coal industry, wrote in 1932: "All the evidence suggests that between the accession of Elizabeth [in 1558] and the Civil War [1642–1651], England, Wales, and Scotland face an acute shortage of wood, which was common to most parts of the island

---

23. Freese, *Coal*, 21–26.

rather than limited to special areas, and which we may describe as a national crisis without laying ourselves open to a charge of exaggeration."[24]

For much of the twentieth century, scholars have taken Nef at his word. In volume one of his *History of the British Coal Industry* (1993), John Hatcher reaffirmed Nef's assertion: "There is strong evidence that an accelerating shortfall in the supply of wood was under way in many of the towns of eastern England early in Elizabeth's reign, and that by the opening decades of the seventeenth century broad swathes of the country were facing a lack of affordable local [wood] firing."[25]

However, recent scholarship has revealed that wood prices actually fell in England from 1550 to 1750. It wasn't a national timber crisis that shoved coal to the forefront of English energy consumption. Instead, an urban timber crisis in London fed the demand for coal, with smaller regional wood shortages in and around large towns also contributing to coal's rising popularity.[26]

What's more, human ecologist Andreas Malm has recently argued that a simple focus on the economic relationship between deforestation and fuelwood price increases fails to account for the changing political climate in which coal use expanded in preindustrial England. In 1566, a royal court that served at the pleasure of Queen Elizabeth I excluded all mineral resources besides gold and silver from Crown control. In essence, virtually anyone wishing to invest capital in coal mining could now do so.

Prior to the edict, the church, which owned the majority of the island's coal-rich lands, offered little incentive to exploit coal. "Merchants were kept at arm's length," argues Malm, and "the bishops and monks were not dependent on the market for their reproduction, hence under no compulsion to increase productivity or reinvest surpluses; thriving on sword and cross, they could afford to stay aloof from subterranean riches." With this dramatic shift in the politics of English property ownership in the middle of the sixteenth century, the merchants of Newcastle, Birmingham, London, and other urban centers who previously limited their activities to *trade* in goods, were quick to venture into the *production* of goods, especially coal.[27]

Changes in Newcastle at the turn of the seventeenth century are instructive about the ways in which the crown's embrace of merchant capitalism (subject to royal taxation, of course) transformed the coal industry. In 1600, a group of forty-eight men calling themselves the Hostmen of Newcastle Upon Tyne applied for

---

24. John Nef, *Rise of the British Coal Industry, Vol. 1* (Hamden: Archon Books, 1966 [1932]), 161.

25. John Hatcher, *History of the British Coal Industry, Volume I* (Oxford: Clarendon Press, 1993), 7.

26. For example, see W. Edward Steinmueller, "The Pre-Industrial Energy Crisis and Resource Scarcity as a Source of Transition," *Research Policy* 42, no. 10 (2013): 1739–48.

27. Malm, *Fossil Capital*, 322.

FIGURE 1.2 The Seale of the Freternity of the Ostmen of the Towne of Newcastle Upon Tine.
Source: Extracts from the *Records of the Company of Hostmen of Newcastle Upon Tyne* (Durham, England: Surtees Society, 1901), https://archive.org/details/extractshostmen00surtuoft. Public Domain.

and received a charter to become the sole purveyors of Newcastle coal to other regions of England and beyond (see Figure 1.2). In the charter, Queen Elizabeth proclaimed:

> Of our speciall grace, certen knowledge, and mere motion, we have given and graunted, and by theis presents for us, our heirs and successors, do geve and graunt, libertie, power, and auethoritie by theis presents, to the said governor and stewards and brethren of the fraternitie of the hostemen of the towne of Newcastle upon Tyne, in the countie of the towne of Newcastle upon Tyne, and their successors, that the governor, stewards, and brethren of the said fraternitie for the time being, and their successors, and everie of them for ever hereafter, shall and may quietlie and peaceablie have, holde, use, and enjoy all and singular such liberties, priviledges, immunities, jurisdictions,

uses, and customes, and everie of them, for and concerning the loadinge and unloadinge, chargeinge and dischargeinge of sea coles, stone coles, and pitt coles, and stones called grindstones, rubstones, and whetstones.[28]

In practice, the Hostmen had already built a monopoly, and the Crown was already taxing Newcastle coal at a rate of one schilling per wagonload. Town officials also received a modest tax from the Hostmen, but the townspeople, who not only consumed but also aspired to trade coal themselves, protested the rising cost of locally mined coal that resulted from the Queen's grant of exclusive powers to the Hostmen. In a 1603 "Complaint of the Maior and Burgesses," the townspeople detested the use of money from the "Common Treasure" to pay for the charter fee, the exclusivity of the "fraternitie of Hostmen," and the highly organized fashion by which the Hostmen crushed any form of competition that might lower prices.[29]

Their complaint mostly fell on deaf ears. In fact, twenty years later, when national sentiment turned against monopolies, King James I approved a law abolishing them, but explicitly exempted the Hostmen of Newcastle Upon Tyne from the ban:

> That this act, or any declaration, provision, penalty, forfeiture, or other thing before mentioned, shall not extend or be prejudicial to any use, custom, privilege, heretofore claimed, used, or enjoyed by the governors and stewards and brethren of the fellowship of the hoast-men of the town of Newcastle upon Tine, or by the antient fellowship, guild, or fraternity commonly called hoastmen, for or concerning the selling, carrying, lading, disposing, shipping, venting, or trading of or for any seacoals, stone-coals, or pit-coals, forth or out of the haven and river of Tine.[30]

In Newcastle, fast becoming Britain's foremost source of coal (see Map 1.1), the interests of local businessmen and national leaders collided with those of ordinary townspeople who witnessed firsthand the astounding wealth generated by the coal trade to which they themselves were not a party. But a simple royal decree, the grant of a charter, a complaint fallen on deaf ears, or an exception

28. "Portion of Queen Elizabeth's Charter to Newcastle upon Tyne, containing the Incorporation of the Hostmen's Company," 1600, in *Extracts from the Records of the Company of Hostmen of Newcastle Upon Tyne* (Durham, UK: Surtees Society, 1901), 15–16, https://archive.org/details/extractshostmen00surtuoft.

29. "The Complaint of the Maior and Burgesses of Newcastle Upon Tyne against the Corporacion of the fraternity of Oastmen of the same Towne," 1603, in *Extracts from the Records of the Company of Hostmen of Newcastle Upon Tyne*, 19, https://archive.org/details/extractshostmen00surtuoft.

30. "Extract from the Statute of Monopolies," 1623, in *Extracts from the Records of the Company of Hostmen of Newcastle Upon Tyne*, 28, https://archive.org/details/extractshostmen00surtuoft.

to an antimonopoly statute, did not allow merchant-capitalists unfettered access to the coal that sat below England's aristocratic manors and church lands. They confronted the political claims of those that actually worked the land above the coal seams.

Centuries of English customary law afforded tenant farmers open use of woodlands for timber and pasturage for animals, so long as they provided the required labor to the landlord. While lords had enclosed portions of their land prior to the edict of 1566, they rarely did so because of the coal that might lie beneath. After the edict however, coal became a primary driver of the enclosure of the English commons. It was the mechanism by which a would-be capitalist could negate any competition for resources from the commoners that lived on the land.

Unsurprisingly, those faced with expulsion or a curtailment of their own economic preferences did not go quietly. In the early seventeenth century, nearly all of the manors recently enclosed in order to extract coal faced violent opposition and sabotage from the freeholders and customary tenants that lived there. For example, on the Sutton manor, which would later become one of the largest collieries (coal mines) in Lancashire, commoners destroyed the enclosures sixteen times. In Shropshire, "local inhabitants waged a stubborn campaign to shut down the collieries, destroying gates, seizing machinery, and stoning [coal] labourers, in a corner of a battlefield stretching across the country."

As we can see from these early battles to control coal, the emerging carbon economy had already transformed English life and politics 150 to 200 years before coal-fired steam engines positioned England to become the unrivaled industrial powerhouse of the world. Those battles would only intensify and spread across the globe as coal and later oil literally fueled European imperialism.

Despite the fervent protests of commoners, coal consumption in England proceeded apace so that by the mid-eighteenth century, all of the necessary features of a full-fledged fossil economy were in place except for the technical capacity to scale up industrial production in an exponential and self-sustaining fashion. In this sense, eighteenth-century England paralleled developments seven centuries before in China.

But coal's relation to the political economy of England looked decidedly different than that which had joined coal to political developments in Song and later Ming and Qing China. In particular, the English state's backing of private investment generated significant accumulation of capital in the hands of colliery owners, transporters, and manufacturers. By allowing colliers to flood local markets with relatively cheap fuel, thereby turning coal into a subsistence commodity akin to fuelwood or even grain, the state indirectly encouraged urbanization. The same process enabled would-be factory owners to consume coal at ever-higher rates provided that the necessary technology to transmit its energy became available. And it was in manufacturing cities like London and in coal production and transport cities like Newcastle where a growing surplus labor supply could readily be turned, even if unwillingly, to work the adjacent mines and factories.[31]

We have seen that prior to the carbon age kicked off by Britain's Industrial Revolution, the carbon economy and the politics that attended it formed a relatively small piece of the overall global energy economy. This economy was in no way an integrated one, instead fragmented into smaller sets of regional relationships and mostly contained within the geographical or political boundaries of single societies. Most turned not to fossil fuels for their energy needs, but instead to the energy afforded them by forests, farming, and careful water management. This was true across societies of wide-ranging sizes from the Haya of Tanzania to Han China. Those that did turn to coal, like Song China and Elizabethan England, did so on scales certainly formidable but without the technological capacity or full political will to move beyond proto-fossil status.

We ought not to assume that either China or England wanted to do so either. Political leaders and ordinary subjects concerned themselves with other kinds of energy matters, including the constant need to maintain irrigation and transport canals in China or the growing demands for coal as a heating and cooking, instead of a manufacturing fuel, in England. Chapter 2 will turn to the ways in which first Britain and soon after other European countries and their settler colonies, along with Japan, moved from a proto-fossil existence fully into the carbon age. We will see how this transition radically altered not just the political relations within industrializing societies but also fundamentally reshaped relations of power across the world.

FURTHER READING

Ball, Philip. *The Water Kingdom: A Secret History of China*. Chicago: University of Chicago Press, 2017.

Elvin, Mark. *The Retreat of the Elephants: An Environmental History of China*. New Haven, CT: Yale University Press, 2004.

Freese, Barbara. *Coal: A Human History*. New York: Penguin, 2003.

Schmidt, Peter R. *Iron Technology in East Africa*. Bloomington: Indiana University Press, 1997.

Williams, Michael. *Deforesting the Earth: From Prehistory to Global Crisis*. Chicago: University of Chicago Press, 2003.

Wrigley, E. A. "Energy and the English Industrial Revolution," *Philosophical Transactions* 371, 1986 (March 2013): 1–10.

---

31. Malm, *Fossil Capital*, 321–25; Peter Stearns, *The Industrial Revolution in World History* (Boulder, CO: Westview Press, 2013), 50.

2 LIFE IN THE FACTORY

Through the mansions of fear, through the mansions of pain
I see my daddy walking through them factory gates in the rain
Factory takes his hearing, factory gives him life
The work, the work, just the working life

—BRUCE SPRINGSTEEN, *"Factory,"* 1978

Industrialization has radically transformed planet Earth and its inhab-itants. But its outcomes and even its very occurrence were in no way preordained. Rather, a series of individual and collective decisions gave shape to the structures, rhythms, and experiences of industrialization, expanded its geographic reach, and shaped the political options and choices available to those involved. As people chose or did not choose one path or another, they in turn shaped industrial life. Historians are still trying to make better sense of why the Industrial Revolution happened when and where it did.

Put simply, industrialization "consisted of the application of new sources of power to the production process, achieved with the transmission equipment necessary to apply this power to manufacturing." Further, it required and then subsequently hastened organization, specialization, and coordination.[1] The new source of power in question in the 1760s when Britain's industrial transition began was coal, whose thermal energy could then be converted to mechanical power by way of the steam engine. By the 1890s, the internal combustion engine made oil's thermal power transferrable into motion. These two carbon fuels reconfigured nearly every aspect of human life.

---

1. Peter Stearns, *The Industrial Revolution in World History* (Boulder, CO: Westview Press, 2013), 6.

The steam engine, however, did not suddenly create a demand for coal in the second half of the eighteenth century. As we saw in chapter 1, that demand already existed in the United Kingdom of Great Britain, which by 1707 consisted of the home nations of England, Scotland, and Wales, and Ireland by 1801 (see Map 2.1). Rather, the growing demand for coal as a heat fuel source prompted inventors to experiment with machinery capable of exploiting harder-to-reach stores of coal, particularly as mine shafts extended below the water table and were subject to regular flooding.

The first attempts to convert coal's thermal power into motion involved burning it to produce steam that in turn drove a piston in a vertical fashion, which then pumped water out of mine shafts. It could not do much else, nor was it intended to. The steam engine's first intentional application was not in manufacturing, but instead to avoid exhausting supplies of relatively cheap heat fuel. But once James Watt successfully tethered coal's concentrated energy to the wheel in 1784 to produce rotative motion, coal's importance to exponential manufacturing was at least within reach.

The technology itself does not, however, explain why coal and steam-driven machines were adopted and popularized in ways that made them common in factories in mid-nineteenth-century Britain and later elsewhere. For carbon-driven technologies to gain traction, there had to be a willingness to use them.

Not until the 1820s did manufacturers in Britain's cotton industry give the steam engine a serious try. Not until the mid-1830s did coal-fired steam power overtake waterpower as the prime mover in Britain's cotton industry—the first to adopt steam on a mass scale. What structural economic and political forces shaped those individual decisions? How did the British government shape and respond to changes in manufacturing? Why did enough people adopt the new technologies so as to make them affordable? How did the experience of industrialization in Britain impact similar transformations elsewhere in the second half of the nineteenth century? For answers to these questions, we must consider both the big structural forces as well as the individual choices that produced industrialization.[2]

Why Britain?

The global impacts of industrialization that extend into the present have sparked intense debate about its central causes. Global approaches to the study of history have, more recently, shaped this discourse. They have rightly call into question the often-repeated claim that the uniqueness of Britain and other parts of northwestern Europe made the region an incubator of technological and economic innovation

---

2. Andreas Malm, *Fossil Capital: The Rise of Steam Power and the Roots of Global Warming* (New York: Verso, 2016), 16–17.

destined to industrialize first. Such claims have more to do with attempts to explain and sometimes justify European economic and political dominance once it emerged by the end of the nineteenth century than with understanding the actual circumstances from which industrialization sprang. Industrialization enabled European ascendancy, not the other way around.

Why did Britain industrialize first, and why did industrialization happen there in the late eighteenth and early nineteenth centuries instead of earlier or later? In the last three decades or so, historians have posited a range of explanations. Some have challenged while others have reinforced earlier or conventional narratives that tend to make Britain seem exceptional. It is worth considering several of these positions, not necessarily to side with one or another, but instead to understand that despite what we think we know about the causes of a process so engrained in our modern lives, the answers are not simple. They require continued historical scrutiny.

Most explanations of Britain's Industrial Revolution incorporate some combination of the following, with varying degrees of emphasis. The first explains the Industrial Revolution as a result of free-market policy. According to this argument, Britain had, by the mid-eighteenth century, internalized a set of market-oriented capitalist principles and corresponding noninterventionist government policies that favored private property and encouraged risk-taking, investment, and technological innovation. Scholars putting forth this argument have often identified England's Glorious Revolution of 1688 as the impetus for these changes. It empowered a market-friendly parliament, checked royal authority, and privileged claims to private property. To put it in more recent terms, by the eighteenth-century Britain had a favorable investment climate.

However, evidence suggests problems with this interpretation. If one examines banking and interest rates before and after 1688, it is hard to detect a marked rise in investment as a result of new English law. Moreover, France and China had similarly favorable investment climates where property rights were concerned but did not industrialize until the late nineteenth and late twentieth centuries, respectively. As historian Peter Stearns notes, "New economic theories helped produce some policies favorable to industrialization, but these did not cause the process; they came too late, and they affected too few people." It is difficult therefore to attribute Britain's industrial success simply to its embrace of capitalism. We might instead think about capitalism as a concurrent development rather than a cause.[3]

A second explanation of Britain's Industrial Revolution emphasizes a rise in literacy and an embrace of science. With literacy rates rising from 6 percent in 1500

---

3. Robert C. Allen, *The British Industrial Revolution in Global Perspective* (Cambridge: Cambridge University Press, 2009), 5; Kenneth Pomeranz, *The Great Divergence: China, Europe, and the Making of the Modern World Economy* (Princeton, NJ: Princeton University Press, 2000), 170; Stearns, *The Industrial Revolution in World History*, 41.

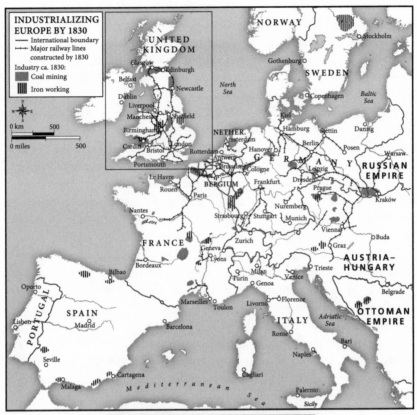

Map 2.1 Industrializing Europe by 1830

to 53 percent in 1800, an increasingly knowledgeable British public had become more receptive to scientific ideas and rational thought than either their medieval relatives or contemporaries living in other, allegedly backward societies. At all levels of industry, from owners to managers to shop floor laborers, a growing adherence to science and its technical applications produced profound efficiency unknown elsewhere. Or so the explanation goes.

But like free-market ideas, such developments were at best conditions or outcomes, not causes of industrialization. Indeed, thinkers generated most of the basic scientific knowledge directly applicable to the coal-fired steam engine before 1700 and did so outside of Britain. By the seventeenth century, for example, Indian intellectuals began to place a high premium on the relationship between knowledge of the natural world and its practical economic applications. Prior to the advent of the power loom, British cloth manufacturers imitated Indian techniques and craftsmanship, not the other way around. Likewise, scientific inquiry, including a more advanced understanding of physics as it related to technology, was just as robust in seventeenth-century France, the Dutch Republic, and Italy as it was in Britain.[4]

Moreover, explanations that equate capitalist-industrial development with rationality (the most famous is German sociologist Max Weber's 1904 *The Protestant Ethic and the Spirit of Capitalism*) tend to assume an absence of rationality in peasant societies. But recent studies of medieval English peasants have revealed the prevalence of rational economic decision-making by the 1380s. At that time, peasant revolts against the lords of the manors initiated a class struggle that ultimately brought about serfdom's formal abolition by 1574. It is hard to see rationality, science, and literacy as causes of the Industrial Revolution. They were useful preconditions to be sure, but in no way destined Britain to become the first industrial powerhouse.[5]

The third explanation stems from an interest in the creation and development of the western nuclear family. Recently, it has served as a case for why northwestern Europe (including Britain) industrialized first, even if it does not fully explain the reasons for when industrialization occurred. From 1650 to 1850, northwestern Europe, including Britain, underwent what historian Jan de Vries has coined an "industrious revolution." This process involved not factories, coal mines, and steam engines but instead nuclear family units whose individual members both responded to and shaped new consumption patterns by reconfiguring household craft production.

Since nuclear families were smaller, and in de Vries's estimation, weaker than extended kinship families found virtually everywhere else in the world, they could

4. Prasannan Parthasarathi, *Why Europe Grew Rich and Asia Did Not* (Cambridge: Cambridge University Press, 2011), 6, 34–35.

5. Allen, *The British Industrial Revolution in Global Perspective*, 7–8.

maneuver more nimbly in relation to market forces like rising fuel prices, variations in rents, or lags in global trade. As such, any surplus a single family might generate could more readily be spent not on the bare essentials but on desired items.

These decisions to purchase nonessentials were not imposed by scheming industrialists eager to extract profits but were the outcome of a set of familial relationships more easily adaptable to individual consumer tastes and fashions. De Vries sites the explosion in popularity of the pocket watch—the seventeenth century's iPhone—as an example. In short, industrialization did not create demand for products. It was one possible, albeit not inevitable response to consumer demands already emerging among relatively small families. This was especially the case in urban areas where increasing access to foreign products further enriched the new consumer culture.[6]

The fourth explanation is closely related to the third. In Britain, this emerging consumerism was particularly pronounced given the relatively high wages earned there when compared to the Dutch Republic, the Southern Netherlands (modern-day Belgium), or France. High wages, coupled with the availability of cheap coal, comprise a fourth potential cause of Britain's Industrial Revolution.

The story goes like this. Following the outbreak of bubonic plague in Britain (1348–1349), population numbers plummeted sharply and then recovered slowly. The long period of steady increase kept wages sufficiently high and increased mobility among agricultural workers, which empowered those rational peasants to destroy serfdom. Britain's subsequent commercial expansion via trade and colonialism in the seventeenth century sustained high wages through urbanization and higher agricultural productivity.

In their quest to curtail growing labor costs, British business owners became more receptive to investment in technology that could do work usually done by humans or animals. But without a cheap supply of coal, technological investments would have amounted to little. Wages did not immediately fall when the steam engine entered first coal mines and then factories. Indeed, cheap coal enabled mine and factory owners to continue to pay relatively high wages to British miners and factory workers through the early nineteenth century, even through, as we will see, the first structural crisis of industrial capitalism in the 1820s.[7] From a purely economic standpoint, this case makes good sense. But we should also be careful not to reduce the cause of such a transformative process like industrialization to the basics of supply and demand within a single economy. This has the result of downplaying the role of the wider world in enabling Britain's revolution.

---

6. Jan de Vries, *The Industrious Revolution: Consumer Behavior and the Household Economy, 1650–Present* (Cambridge: Cambridge University Press, 2008), 1–19; Allen, *Britain's Industrial Revolution in Global Perspective*, 12–13.

7. Allen, *The British Industrial Revolution in Global Perspective*, 15.

A fifth explanation further de-centers Britain and Western Europe as unique technological innovators. It situates the Industrial Revolution more firmly within the realm of global trade. Britain's foray into global trade in the seventeenth century via the forced acquisition of colonial territory not only freed access to raw materials and new markets for British wares. It also spurred the growth of a consumer culture in which participants now worked harder and more efficiently in order to afford the goods increasingly available to them. Within this context, an emphasis on Britain's high wages begins to make more sense.

In the last three decades or so, historians have begun to understand more fully the impacts of these interdependent processes of colonialism, trade, consumerism, and industrialization. Kenneth Pomeranz has argued that on the eve of what would become Britain's Industrial Revolution in the 1760s, it had little economic advantage in terms of capital, consumerism, or technological prowess as China or Japan, for example.

What it did have though, in concert with France and the Dutch Republic, were colonial territories in the Americas and a relatively steady supply of forced, unpaid labor from Africa with which to grow or extract cotton, sugar, minerals, timber, and other materials required to scale up production to industrial levels. This prevented Britain from having to "mobilize huge numbers of additional workers who would have been needed to use [Britain's] own land in much more intensive and ecologically sustainable ways."[8] In short, what ultimately gave Britain and other Western European countries a leg up on the other eighteenth-century workshops of the world like China, Japan, India, and the Ottoman Empire, were its vast holdings in North America and the Caribbean.

Like these other explanations, simply having overseas colonies was not on its own sufficient to cause the Industrial Revolution. Later, we will explore further the ways in which Europe's colonial expansions in the nineteenth century intersected with its increased reliance on coal and oil and rendered colonialism and energy production interdependent. But for now, we ought not to see European colonialism in the seventeenth and eighteenth centuries in the Americas, like any of the aforementioned conditions, as the sole cause of industrialization. Rather, colonialism served as perhaps one of the most critical preconditions for industrialization. But it still did not make industrialization inevitable.

Each of these big, structural processes help us understand the changes that led to industrialization. None of them on their own were sufficient to cause the Industrial Revolution, but together they made, in hindsight, industrialization more likely to have occurred first in Britain and thereafter other parts of Western Europe, as opposed to somewhere else or at a different time.

Nothing about these structural changes was preordained. They involved the collective decisions of all kinds of people, which we will now turn to in order to

---

8. Pomeranz, *The Great Divergence*, 264.

better understand how structure and agency informed each other, particularly in the realm of the politics of carbon energy and the technologies it powered during Britain's industrial shift.

Slow Steam, Rushing Water

In the early 1780s, James Watt faced a problem. Few people were buying his steam engine. His invention marked a vast improvement in efficiency and fuel consumption over the work of Thomas Newcomen. Newcomen's steam pump, patented in 1712, served primarily to pump water out of underground coal and tin mines in England and Scotland. While certainly innovative, Newcomen's device required that it be used adjacent to coal pit mines so as not to incur high transport costs for the vast amounts of fuel required to power the reciprocating pump. Watt's separate condenser (patented 1769) cut fuel use by one-third and allowed for the steam-driven reciprocating pump to be used where coal reserves were less plentiful. But by the early 1780s, orders for his steam engine had slowed to a trickle.

At the urging of his business partner Matthew Boulton, Watt returned to the workshop and applied steam power to a new device that generated rotative motion rather than the simple linear up-and-down of the reciprocating pump (see Figure 2.1).

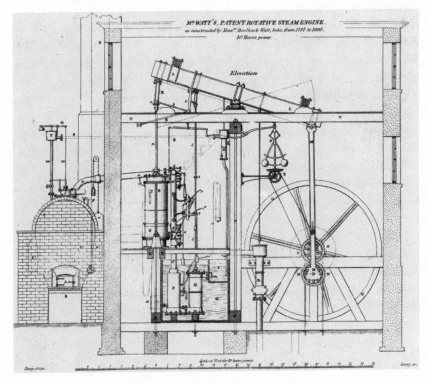

FIGURE 2.1 Technical drawing of a Watt steam engine, 1787.
Source: Science and Society Picture Library

Boulton saw the future, apparently: "There is no other Cornwall [a reference to tin mining] to be found and the most likely line for consumption of our engines is the application of them to mills which is certainly an extensive field."[9]

Boulton & Watt was however, swimming against the current, so to speak. Cornmeal grinders and cotton spinners—representatives of the first two mill industries the duo targeted with sales pitches and demonstrations—really liked water. Take for example the Robinson brothers of Nottinghamshire, who owned several cotton-spinning factories on the river Leen. Always keen to try the latest technical innovations in milling, the Robinsons ordered a Boulton & Watt rotative steam engine in 1784, and by 1786, coal powered a portion of their spinning mules when the river's flow was weak. But the brothers complained incessantly of the high cost of fuel, and their technical investments over the next decade primarily went to modernizing their waterpower capabilities instead of switching to coal. They sold the second of the two Boulton & Watt engines they had purchased just a year later.

Boulton & Watt sold about a dozen steam engines to cotton manufacturers by 1790. But most entrepreneurs of the time leveled similar complaints as the Robinsons. They, along with Richard Arkwright and Robert Owen, two other wildly successful cotton-spinning manufacturers of the late eighteenth century, all tried coal-fired steam power. They decided it was inferior to the free and reliable river's flow. In 1807, a friend of Watt remarked that "In all mills it is necessary that considerable power be employed in order to accomplish the intended purpose. Water is the most common power, and indeed the best, as being the most constant and equable . . . Mills may also be moved by the force of steam . . . but the expense of fuel must undoubtedly prevent this mode of construction mills from ever becoming general."[10]

It is not the case that Boulton & Watt closed the century as complete failures. By 1800, they had exported twenty-five engines for use in Dutch, French, Spanish, and Russian mills. Manufacturers widely recognized steam as a technically sound alternative to water. But given the rather obvious cost limitations when compared to waterpower, why then did manufacturers ever adopt coal-fired steam on a large scale at all?

To answer this question, we need to consider several key political developments in the British economy in the first three decades of the nineteenth century. These developments, only when combined, prompted many cotton manufacturers to seriously consider adopting steam power as the prime mover of mechanized production.

---

9. Quoted in Malm, *Fossil Capital*, 54.

10. John Robinson, *Encyclopaedia Perthensis, The New Encyclopedia; Or, Universal Dictionary of Arts and Sciences*, Vol. 13 (London, 1807), 154, quoted in Malm, *Fossil Capital*, 56.

The first development had to do with the British government's and factory owners' attempts to repress worker mobilization at the moment the factory system emerged. In 1800, Parliament passed the second of two Combination Laws, the first of which had passed the year before but was repealed upon passage of the second. The Combination Law of 1800 made illegal any attempt by workers to form or join a union for the purposes of collectively bargaining with their employers over wages, hours, quantity of work, or conditions of safety. Any disputes between "workmen" and "masters" was to be meted out through arbitration before a royally appointed justice of the Peace. Masters could serve as justices in disputes outside of their respective trade. For example, a cotton manufacturer could serve as an arbiter in a conflict between a collier and a mine owner, but not between a cotton spinner and a fellow cotton manufacturer. The architects of the law could claim impartiality in this sense. But workers were not permitted to serve as justices too. Thus, their influence within this system remained dispersed and weak. Their only formal entrée into arbitration was as a plaintiff up against the monied interests of their local communities. These interests were increasingly willing to defend their growing profits at all costs.[11]

During Britain's water-powered cotton boom then, the government took an active role in ensuring that production levels increased or at least remained steady. It did so by empowering manufacturers to the detriment of workers. If they perceived parliament not to have gone far enough in protecting their interests, manufacturers took matters into their own hands. As one critic observed in 1818, "There is an abominable combination existing amongst the masters, first established at Stockport [near Manchester] in 1802, and it has since become so general, as to embrace all the great masters for a circuit of many miles round Manchester...They are the most obnoxious beings ... that can be imagined ... When the combination first took place, one of their first articles was, that no master should take on [employ] a man until he had first ascertained whether his last master had discharged him."[12] If it turned out to be the case that the master and worker could not agree on wages, it was unlikely the worker could find employment at another mill or shop in the vicinity.

The second development was in part a response to the first. Perhaps unsurprisingly, the Combination Laws emboldened radical political organizing among workers. Rather than curb or eliminate union activity, the laws simply drove it underground. Empowered by the revolutionary ideas of *liberté*, *égalité*, and *fraternité*

---

11. *Statutes at Large,* (39 and 40 Geo. III, c. 106), LIII, pp. 847–62; in A. Aspinall and E. Anthony Smith, eds., *English Historical Documents, XI, 1783–1832* (New York: Oxford University Press, 1959), 749–52.

12. A Journeyman Cotton Spinner, "Address to the public of strike-bound Manchester," 1818, quoted in E. P. Thompson, *The Making of the English Working Class* (New York: Vintage, 1966), 200.

unleashed in the 1790s in neighboring France, British workers forged a clear sense of their political activities as wrapped up in their economic livelihood. The growing reliance on self-acting spinning mules, power looms, and other machines that required less human skill to operate than, for example, cloth-weaving using hand tools, further exacerbated these class tensions. Seemingly in anticipation of the Combination Laws to come a few years later, the radical author John Thelwall observed in 1796 in *The Rights of Nature*:

> The fact is, that monopoly, and the hideous accumulation of capital in a few hands, like all diseases not absolutely mortal, carry, in their own enormity, the seeds of cure. Man is, by his very nature, social and communicative—proud to display the little knowledge he possesses, and eager, as opportunity presents, to increase his store. Whatever presses men together, therefore, though it may generate some vices, is favourable to the diffusion of knowledge, and ultimately promotive of human liberty. Hence every large workshop and manufactory is a sort of political society, which no act of parliament can silence, and no magistrate disperse.[13]

It was not simply cotton factory hands that formed the crux of this emerging working-class consciousness from the 1790s through the 1840s. As historian E. P. Thompson reminds us: "In many towns the actual nucleus from which the labour movement derived ideas, organisation, and leadership, was made up of such men as shoemakers, weavers, saddlers and harnessmakers, booksellers, printers, building workers, small tradesmen, and the like . . . The vast area of Radical London between 1815 and 1850 drew its strength from no major heavy industries . . . but from the host of smaller trades and occupations."

These skilled artisans and craftsmen met in taverns, homes, and in the backs of workshops to share radical literature, organize work stoppages, maintain craft traditions, and simply participate in a community of like-minded people with shared political and economic interests. Thompson has called this development the making of the English working class—with an emphasis on the singular class—because this consciousness brought together men (a glaring blind spot in Thompson's analysis that excluded women) from a variety of industries and trades. They began to see themselves as distinct from other members of their community whose economic and political power was, on the surface, much greater.[14]

---

13. John Thelwall, *The Rights of Nature Against the Usurpations of Establishments,* (London: H. D. Symonds, 1796), 21.

14. Thompson, *The Making of the English Working Class,* 193–94. For a notable critique of Thompson, see "Women in *The Making of the English Working Class,*" in Joan Scott, *Gender and the Politics of History* (New York: Columbia University Press, 1999), 68–90.

This growing working class consciousness manifest itself in a variety of ways throughout Britain from the passage of the Combination Law of 1800 to its repeal in 1824. In the early nineteenth century, Scottish weavers petitioned Parliament for minimum wage legislation. On the heels of a particularly gruesome depression in 1811, artisan weavers united across Scotland and northern England, including a seven-week strike in western Scotland to force local magistrates to fix cloth prices. The sheriff responded by ordering the arrest and imprisonment of the leaders of the Glasgow Weavers' Committee in early 1813. Three years later, reformist elements within the weavers' network (which extended beyond the cloth trade) petitioned for labor reforms, and the state responded by putting the Reformers on trial in 1817. The failure of these two strategies employed by workers—one through work stoppage, the other through constitutional petition—resulted in an increasing political radicalism that culminated in the "Radical War" of 1820, when local (illicit) unions armed themselves against state authorities and called for a general strike.[15]

In England, similar developments were afoot. In 1808, the House of Commons rejected a minimum wage petition from weavers that contained 130,000 signatures. Strikes, rebellions, and machine sabotage ensued. In Manchester, workers forced a mill owner to his knees and compelled him to sign a minimum wage agreement. In the Midland manufacturing districts of Nottinghamshire, Yorkshire, and Lancashire, frame-knitters, or stockingers, who produced primarily woolen hosiery, protested the wage cuts and layoffs that resulted in part from Napoleon Bonaparte's economic blockade of Britain. The blockade dropped exports to the United States from 11 million pounds in 1810 to less than 2 million in 1811. A series of poor harvests from 1809 to 1812 drove up the price of bread, making the concurrent loss of work even more devastating. In 1811, small, organized bands of frame-knitters took to disabling or smashing frames—the industrial machinery that symbolized, but did not directly cause, their misery.

Sabotage spread through the Midland districts in a relatively targeted and systematic way (see Figure 2.2). For example, the Luddites, named after their proclaimed leader Ned Ludd, avoided standard frames and went for the wide frames, which produced simpler, cheap stockings at a faster rate, often with the cheaper labor of women or children. Luddites avoided framing houses where owners had not decreased wages or where "frames were making fully fashioned stockings at the proper price." Though slow to care or act, Parliament eventually heeded the complaints of Midlands manufacturers by declaring frame-breaking a capital offense in March 1812.[16]

---

15. Tony Clarke and Tony Dickson, "Class and Class Consciousness in Early Industrial Capitalism: Paisley 1770–1850," in *Capital and Class in Scotland*, ed. Tony Dickson (Edinburgh: John Donald Publishers, 1982), 33–42.

16. Brian Bailey, *The Luddite Rebellion* (New York: New York University Press, 1998), 15, 22, 41–43.

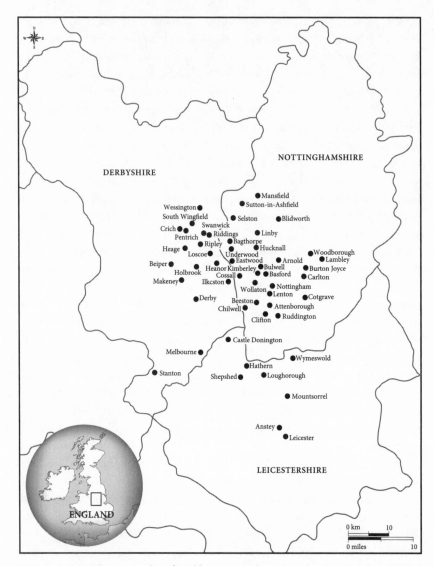

FIGURE 2.2 The geography of Luddite riots and machine-breaking in the Midland counties, 1811–1816.

One might assume because of the sheer number of strikes and the passion-ate nature of workers' political organizing that the early decades of the Industrial Revolution spelled disaster for profits. Quite the opposite. By 1820, the cotton industry entered a period of dynamic growth previously unknown in Britain. Facilitated by access to quick and easy credit from London banks, factory owners in Britain made steep investments in the latest water technology and in spinning mules and power looms. A few supplemented waterpower with steam power, but typically only when proximity to coal reserves warranted. The result was astounding growth in the global cotton trade in the first two decades of the nineteenth century. Having no land or climatic conditions suitable for local growing, British merchants acquired raw cotton from abroad: from the the slave-holding American South, from India via the British East India Company, and by 1821, from Egypt.

A third development, despite manufacturers' optimism in the early 1820s, soon dashed profits and initiated the most sustained battle between capitalists and workers in nineteenth-century Britain. In December 1825 the bubble burst, and the first protracted crisis of industrial capitalism began. A frenzy of factory expansions, innovations in waterpower, mechanization, cheap credit, and a nonunionized workforce largely held down wages. But overproduction by manufacturers and over speculation by investors reached a head. Supply outstripped demand, prices plummeted, and profits disappeared. To make matters worse for the manufacturing class, the cotton bubble created a ripple effect in other British industries as well, including iron production, linen draping, building construction, and investment banking.

Eighteen months before the cotton bubble burst, parliament repealed the ineffective Combination Laws and legalized trade unions. Critics found the laws outright counterproductive because they had prevented workers from bringing forth reasonable complaints or policy requests. They drove many workers to radicalism. And in any case, profits were soaring.

Before the panic of 1825, manufacturers could afford to pay higher wages relative to other areas of Europe and still make a killing. The repeal did not end trade unionism but instead accelerated it straight through the economic crisis. From at least late 1825, desperation drove workers' political activism, including the Chartist movement (1838) for universal male suffrage and substantial changes in the parliamentary election process. By the general strike of 1842, Britain was on the brink of all-out revolution.[17]

The desperation cut across lines of gender and race. Women played active roles in a range of protest movements, including food riots, antienclosure demonstrations, and protests against the New Poor Law (1834), which severely restricted access to government poverty assistance.[18] William Cuffay, whose grandfather had toiled in slavery on the British-ruled Caribbean island of St. Kitts, joined the Chartist movement in 1839, and became one of the most militant and highly regarded of its London-based leadership. Though small in number, black Britons had already formed important connections between working class and antislavery activism that exposed the dependence of Britain's manufacturing class on the raw materials produced throughout the empire.[19]

---

17. Malm, *Fossil Capital*, 59–61.

18. Neville Kirk, *Labour and Society in Britain and the USA, Vol. 1: Capitalism, Custom and Protest, 1780–1850* (Brookfield, VT: Ashgate, 1994), 120.

19. Ron Ramdin, *The Making of the Black Working Class in Britain* (Brookfield, VT: Gower, 1987), 25–26.

Journalists and other observers who visited mill towns and urban manufacturing districts expressed horror at the anxiety, filth, disease, and starvation that pushed working families to the brink. Writing in 1833, surgeon Peter Gaskell described the rapidly declining fortunes of British weavers:

> Although famine and cold, and supplications for bread from the mouths of his children — although feebleness and hunger, and overstrained exertion— have been the lot of the hand-loom weaver, it is of late only that he has begun to feel that he was reduced to extremity; that his contest with steam production was a vain one; that it had ground him to the dust, and must ultimately either starve him into outrage, or force him to quit his country ... [He] is exchanging his labour for a price utterly inadequate to supply the commonest wants of humanity.[20]

Similarly, the German observer Friedrich Engels, who with Karl Marx penned *The Communist Manifesto* (1848), described in 1844 the conditions of children in factory districts:

> The high mortality among children of workers, particularly factory workers, is sufficient proof of the unhealthy conditions under which their early years are spent. These unfavourable factors naturally affect also those children who manage to survive, but not unscathed. The very least that they suffer is ill health, arrested development, and general constitutional weakness ... Such a child is not likely to have the same capacity for labour as one brought up in healthier surroundings.[21]

It was in this triple context of severe economic depression, dire health and sanitary conditions, and a flowering class consciousness among workers and owners alike, that coal-fired steam power—as Gaskell suggested—overtook waterpower and transformed Britain into the central hub of fossil-fueled industrial production. And the shift to carbon energy ultimately occurred in part because of a counterintuitive problem: human labor was too cheap!

Here's how it unfolded. The 1824 repeal of the Combination Law created a spike in union activity. At least at the beginning of the structural crisis, unionized workers blocked wage cuts that manufacturers claimed as absolutely necessary. Indeed, Manchester cotton spinners' wages reached a peak of 30 shillings a week in

20. Peter Gaskell, *Artisans and Machinery: The Moral and Physical Condition of the Manufacturing Population* (London: John W. Parker, 1833), 44.

21. Friedrich Engels, *The Condition of the Working Class in England*, trans. and ed. W. O. Henderson and W. H. Chaloner (Stanford, CA: Stanford University Press, 1958), 169.

1831, six years after the panic set in. But as the crisis deepened, workers in a variety of industries fought not just wage cuts but mass unemployment.

Faced with the degraded circumstances described by Gaskell, Engels, and others, cotton weavers across Britain took to embezzling on a grand scale after the panic of 1825, at the same time that their counterparts in spinning saw their collective union power soar. It was not the first time that weavers had stashed away small amounts of thread to weave into cloth and sell on the black market. But the panic made this tactic even more attractive to weavers struggling to feed their families.

Herein lies the irony. Because piece rate wages paid for woven cloth were so low, desperate weavers embezzled thread either for the first time or more than they might have in years past. In response, manufacturers consolidated oversight of workers and replaced weavers with power looms. The result was the combined factory: the twinned processes of cotton spinning and cotton weaving brought together under one roof and performed by spinning mules and power looms respectively. Unskilled "tenders," often women and children, replaced skilled, mostly male artisans. And coal and steam increasingly replaced water as the prime mover of machines.

But if the reasons for the desire of manufacturers to impose greater oversight and regularity over their human workforce are relatively clear, again why steam and not water? Through the transition years and beyond—indeed as late as 1870—water remained not only cheaper but on average more powerful in terms of its output measured in horsepower than coal. Allen's argument about rising labor costs and cheap fuel is, in this light, only partially correct. The factory system could have just as easily consolidated after the Panic of 1825 on the flow of water. Why did it not? The answer, Malm points out, lies not in the rationality of economics but in the emotional pettiness of the owners.[22]

The year before the structural crisis unleashed its fury, Robert Thom, who worked as what we would today call a hydraulic engineer, submitted a full report on a massive waterworks plan to Michael Shaw, a local lord in Greenock, Scotland, which as it turns out was the birthplace of James Watt, inventor of the rotative steam engine. Greenock was, in Thom's mind, to become the preeminent model for how to scale up the power of water and to eliminate its weather-related irregularities.

As shown in Figure 2.3, Shaws' Waterworks was an intricate system of aqueducts, dams, embankments, reservoirs, self-acting sluices (for regulating water levels), and of course massive water wheels for converting the flow into rotative motion at the sites of would-be mills. It opened to "great fanfare" in 1827, and for the next decade or so, served as a model for other investors serious about transforming the cotton industry not with coal but with water. Plans to develop similar waterworks on the Irwell and Tames rivers—both home to dense clusters of water-powered mills—made their way to investors and Parliament in the early 1830s.

---

22. Malm, *Fossil Capital*, 74.

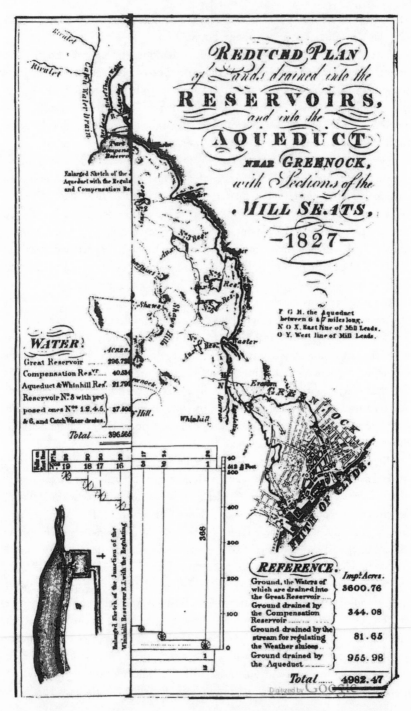

FIGURE 2.3 Reduced Plan of Lands drained into the Reservoirs and into the Aqueduct Near Greenock with Sections of the Mill Seats, 1827.

Source: *A Brief Account of Shaws Water Scheme and Present State of the Works* (Greenock, Scotland: The Columbian Press, 1829). Public Domain.

None of the plans ever came to fruition. At Greenock, only eleven mills oper-ated by the mid-1840s. The reason? Most mill owners could not fathom a system in which their prime source of power rested collectively, involved rate payments (much like a water utility today), or might benefit their competitor either more than them or even at all:

> All indications are ... that the mill-owners fell afoul of the [waterworks] projects because of their unwillingness or inability to submit to the plan-ning, coordination, and collective funding required for the expansion of waterpower capacity on this scale. Some foresaw no private benefit and so did not wish to pay. Some, prey to the constant antagonism between down-stream and upstream factories, expected interruptions of their flow from other mills; some objected to the centralisation of authority. In all these cases, the opposition stemmed from the fact that river management —for the good of the mill-owners as a group—demanded that they step into the shoes of their neighbours.

In this sense, the very nature of water, cycling through weather systems, flowing over varied terrain, constantly in motion, made it very different than coal, which could be cut, carted, and stashed away from competitors. Coal, in other words, freed manufacturers from the constraint of the commons: systems of resource man-agement that checked, even to a small degree, cut-throat competition.

Scaling up waterpower to the levels required for exponential productive capac-ity was not cost prohibitive. Instead it was emotionally prohibitive for many mill owners. With coal, as Malm puts it, "the fire was his own." Percentages corrobo-rate this timeline. In the mid-1830s, coal and water constituted equal power inputs in the cotton industry. On the heels of a short-lived boom that ended in 1838, coal surpassed water, and by 1850 coal and the steam engines that it fed made up 82 percent of total power.[23]

We have now seen that initially the rise of the British factory system did not rest on the rational adoption of cheap coal and reliable steam technology. Both played parts, to be sure, but once the rotative steam engine appeared in 1784, it took until the period between 1834 and 1838 for coal to surpass waterpower as the prime mover of industrial production, a span of at least fifty years. A series of political developments, not raw economics, drove the transition to carbon energy. Indeed, if economics were the only consideration, Britain's mill owners would have coveted waterpower at least into the 1870s.

Instead, faced with an increasingly militant labor force whose prospects for basic necessities seemed to dwindle with each onslaught of capitalism's structural crisis, and the apparently unthinkable possibility of collectivizing waterpower in order to return to times of escalating profits, manufacturers turned to coal. Only

---

23. Malm, *Fossil Capital*, 80, 96–119.

coal allowed them to at once stamp out the irregularities of their human work-force in a methodical and rational sense by reducing most work to machine-tending (which could have also been done with water) *and* to avoid any sort of coordination with their fellow owners that required them to share water power or worse, subsidize their competition, even if it proved cost-beneficial. By 1850, coal, not water, appeared the most appropriate, if irrational fuel source for British capital.

In this chapter's final section, we turn to how coal's slow ascendency in Britain inaugurated a series of political and economic transformations and counterreactions after 1850 in France and Japan—two markedly different societies but linked historically by their relatively rapid, concurrent shifts to industrialization by the turn of the twentieth century. These were not the only places to which industrialization spread after 1850, and in both, aspects of coal extraction and large-scale manufacturing were already underway beforehand.

But the adoption of carbon-fueled industrialization on large scales in these geographically adjacent or economically linked places was no doubt shaped by the technological innovations and growing pains developed and experienced in Britain in the first half of the nineteenth century. The result was that each new round of industrialization carried with it local particularities that shaped how workers, capitalists, and government officials engaged with, shaped, and responded to new industrial realities. None was a carbon copy (again, pun intended) of Britain's example.

Coal Fire Spreads

In 1861, upon news from Paris that the railway would extend to their small city, the residents of Saint-Girons in southwestern France celebrated in the streets with cannon fire and parades. Five years later the Saint-Giron station opened, and the rails that now linked the once sleepy agricultural town and soon after others like it to the main arteries of French commerce and industry began to turn "peasants into Frenchmen."[24] A flurry of road-building linked small villages to larger towns that had train stations, and then on to urban and industrial centers like Paris, Bordeaux, Flanders, and Marseilles. People, goods, and ideas quickly took to the roads and rails.

The rise of France's carbon economy after 1850 was in no small part the result of centralized government planning for a national rail network begun in 1842. Unlike in Britain where government officials saw their role as to invoke eminent domain for private capital, the French government employed workers to build the railways, and then turned over most of the lines to private operators on ninety-nine-year leases.[25] As Figure 2.4 shows, the result was to link short regional clusters of tracks to nearly all corners of the country.

---

24. Eugen Weber, *Peasants Into Frenchmen: The Modernization of Rural France, 1870–1914* (Stanford, CA: Stanford University Press, 1976), 205.

25. Stearns, *The Industrial Revolution in World History*, 58.

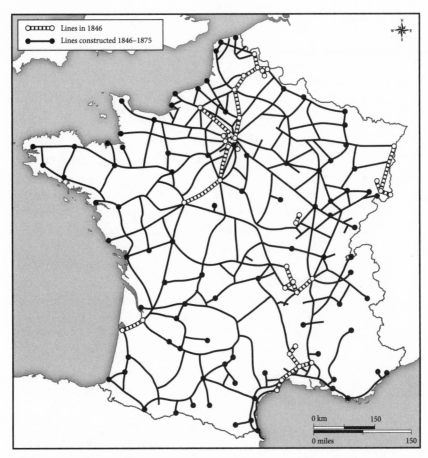

FIGURE 2.4 French rail expansion, 1846–1875.

The extension of rail transport into the French countryside also facilitated an embrace of coal for heavy and light industry alike. Railways drove down the cost of coal transport, which in France, unlike in Britain, did not benefit from a network of densely interconnected, reliable waterways. Coal consumption rose from 7.5 million tons in 1850 to 21 million tons in 1869. The greatest beneficiaries were iron makers, who could now afford cheap coke, and the purveyors of steam engines, the numbers of which rose from 5,200 in 1848 to 32,006 in 1875. It took about as long as it did in Britain, but coal eventually overtook waterpower in industries like spinning and weaving so that by 1906, steam accounted for 78 percent of manufacturing horsepower.[26]

Rail and steam brought about dramatic transformations in work, migration, and socialization that in turn changed people's political engagement at local and

---

26. Roger Price, *A Social History of Nineteenth Century France* (London: Hutchinson, 1987), 38–39.

national levels. As we will explore more in the next chapter, miners and rail workers became essential to working class resistance to corporate paternalism and state-sponsored liberal capitalism.

As goods coursed more frequently along the expanding network of rail lines, so too did people displaced by geographic shifts in the economy. Far and away the largest sector of French industry in 1850, rural handicraft producers who worked at home saw their representation in the industrial workforce drop to 28 percent of the whole by 1906. Railways made it easier for owners to concentrate production near fuel sources or in growing urban centers where cheaper labor and fuel were evermore available.[27]

Though by no means uniform across all regions of France or in all industries, virtually all kinds of workers, from small farmers to skilled artisans to domestics to miners to office clerks, faced fundamental life changes. For example, in 1857, a twenty-seven-year-old unmarried textile worker and mother of two from Amiens dropped her youngest at the local foundling hospital (for "unwanted" children). As she explained: "Why do I send this little child to the hospital; because I am without any resources . . . but I don't want him to be lost for good . . . I beg you to have the kindness to keep him there, so I can see him again when I can, because I am not married."

Her plight was indicative of the changing relations of women to work vis-a-vis industrialization. The centralization of production in urban, coal-fired factories dislocated many workers, but especially women, from rural life where production occurred in the home in tandem with other tasks like childrearing, cooking, and farming.

Similar upheavals had attended Britain's mechanization frenzy in the first half of the nineteenth century. While some women struggled successfully to remain engaged in this kind of economy, more found it increasingly difficult to maintain such ties. The new realities of urbanization and industrialization in turn transformed women's relationship to political organizing. "Communal laundries and streets [of manufacturing districts] were women's [spaces] and it was here that solidarities of gender enabled women to contest high rents and prices, to find new economic strategies, or to seek support in domestic difficulties," as one historian writes.[28]

Such women were not always successful in changing their material conditions through organizing, but their growing presence on the factory floor and on urban streets became the object of inquiry by political economists who sought to explain and shape, through policy, the social and moral upheavals wrought by industrialization.

---

27. Price, *A Social History*, 199.

28. Peter McPhee, *A Social History of France, 1789–1914* (New York: Palgrave Macmillan, 2004), 193–94.

Writing in 1860, Jules Simon, an esteemed member of *La Société d'Economie Politique* (Society of Political Economy) and future legislator during the Third Republic (1870 to 1940), examined what he considered the degraded moral state of French working women, a number of whom, he noted, had turned to part-time prostitution. In the context of a political debate about a free trade agreement with Britain, Simon warned that opening trade with Britain, long an economic rival of France, would eradicate any hope of restoring feminine ideals to French women. According to Simon, women would be evermore rapidly torn from the safe and suitable confines of the home and thrust into the depraved world of factory work.

Rather than question what most political economists of the time considered to be the "natural" law of women's lower economic value, Simon reinforced it. Rather than call into question how capitalist markets functioned, Simon instead lamented the loss of an idealized femininity that had not in fact existed in practical terms among working-class French families. As his contemporary critics noted, Simon failed to offer any practical political solutions to the problems that working women faced or were perceived to face.

In contrast, Julie Daubié, a lesser known political economist and self-described feminist, wrote with policy prescriptions in mind. Daubié was particularly concerned with addressing women's poverty. She identified two root causes: the historical exclusion of women from male-dominated trades (like printing or weaving) to which women's intellect and bodies were in fact perfectly suited, and men's selfish embrace of individual pursuits (like drinking and whoring) at the expense of their societal obligation to maintaining strong, productive families.

Daubié shared with Simon an assumption that "equated immorality and disorganization with the loss of clear lines of sexual difference" as they related to wages and the value of work. But she also advanced practical solutions to the problems faced by working women in industrial France, including legislation that secured equal wages. As historian Joan Scott describes, "Equality, in Daubié's view, would not eradicate sexual difference; it would put women in a position to protect themselves" by enabling single women to support themselves and their children through their wage earnings.[29]

The transformation of the relationship of women to work was of course not the only consequence of French industrialization. Nor was it solely a French development. Women were equally integral to debates and changes that stemmed from carbon-fueled industrialization in Britain and later in places like the United States, Germany, Russia, and Japan. What it does though is highlight the extent of coal's influence by the second half of the nineteenth century. The extension of railways and the rise of factory districts was not just about integrating and growing the national economy to compete across the English Channel. As it had in Britain, carbon

---

29. Scott, *Gender and the Politics of History*, 139–63.

energy transformed social relationships and caused French intellectuals to grapple with a crisis of national ideals, even if those ideals were never or seldom reality.

From its outset, industrialization in Japan was almost completely a political project of the government. In 1872, the newly restored Meiji government (r. 1868–1912) announced the opening of Japan's first rail line between Tokyo and the port of Yokohama. The extension of similar lines in the decades that followed were critical to Meiji plans for political and economic consolidation that also involved telegraph lines (1869), a postal system (1871), universal public education (1871), support for foreign trade, and subsidies for industrial production.

In the early years, a national rail network allowed the Meiji state to more easily deploy its military to pacify local rebellions. Railroads also supported efforts to scale up domestic industry and facilitate the movement of foods like rice and wheat, manufactured products like silk clothing, and of course workers. From 1870 to 1874, railroad construction comprised almost a third of the state's financial outlays for modernization projects. By 1893, Japan had over 2,000 miles of track. As in Europe, railroads became central to industrialization and nation-building.[30]

Among the primary beneficiaries of Japan's burgeoning rail network was the coal industry. Two coalfields in particular, whose production and consumption had remained mostly local during the Tokugawa shogunate (r. 1600–1868) and early Meiji, expanded dramatically once the government enticed private capital to extend lines. Beginning in 1891, coal mined in the fields at Chikuhō in northern Kyushu traveled by rail instead of riverboat to the ports of Wakamatsu and Moji, where it could be loaded onto short-range shipping liners bound for Kansai (see Map 3.1). Output at Chikuhō increased from under one million tons when the rail line opened to almost six-and-a-half million tons in 1906. Rail transport came to dominate the total movement of goods (not just coal) between Chikuhō and its nearby ports, accounting for 84 percent by 1906.

In Jōban too, coal production soared after the Nippon Railway Company replaced the local tracks built by the Iwaki Coal-Mining Company in the 1880s with a direct extension line to Tokyo in 1897. With an annual output of 300,000 tons in 1895, Iwaki's output tripled over the next four years, shipping costs fell by more than 25 percent, and demand for coal as a power source for steam-driven manufacturing surged. What's more, the railroads themselves demanded ever-greater quantities of fuel coal as more locomotives carrying more freight and passenger cars appeared both in Japan's urban areas and the more remote countryside, where surplus rice yields could be efficiently carried to cities by rail.[31]

---

30. Mikoso Hane, *Modern Japan: A Historical Survey* (Boulder: Westview Press, 1996), 98; Stearns, *The Industrial Revolution*, 139; Steven J. Ericson, *The Sound of the Whistle: Railroads and the State in Meiji Japan* (Cambridge, MA: Harvard University Press, 1996), 10, 97.

31. Ericson, *The Sound of the Whistle*, 41–42.

The decision of the Meiji Emperor's ministers to aggressively pursue carbon-fueled industrialization was only partially driven by a desire to modernize the country and to banish Japan's decentralized feudal system to the past. It was also in no small part informed by the very real threat of Western colonialism. To be sure, the two considerations were intertwined. In 1858, the Tokugawa shogunate, under threat of foreign naval vessels anchored off the coast, begrudgingly signed the Ansei Treaties. Commonly known as the "unequal treaties," first demanded by American officials and then shortly thereafter by British, Russian, Dutch, and French envoys, the Ansei Treaties granted foreign signatories access to five treaty ports, fixed low tariff rates, and established rights of extraterritoriality whereby foreigners who committed crimes while in Japan would instead be tried in their home country. While the latter was humiliating and compromised Japan's legal sovereignty, the former proved the most prohibitive of Japan's ability to generate national economic growth. Competition from cheaper imports at specified, western-dominated ports of entry stifled domestic industrial development.[32]

Following the humiliating Ansei Treaties, a small group of samurai lost confidence in the Tokugawa's ability to fend off western incursions. These samurai staged a coup d'état and restored the largely ceremonial Meiji emperor in 1868, effectively ending six hundred years of shogunate rule. While commonly called the Meiji "restoration" because of the emperor's return to Tokyo, the event was more of a revolution, as it transformed in radical ways Japan's legal, political, economic, and social institutions.[33]

Meiji officials immediately sought ways around the limitations of the treaty port system. As shown in Figure 2.5, key to this strategy was to open alternative ports that were not subject to the terms of the Ansei treaties. The first five opened by imperial decree in 1889, and another seventeen opened by 1900. In these special trading ports, as they became known, the Meiji government could impose tariffs and incentivize Japanese merchants to export local goods by chartering foreign (mostly British) vessels and restrict or facilitate trade in nearly any manner it saw fit. These "open ports" afforded Japan the ability to eventually dominate trade with Korea and Taiwan, the latter of which Japan formally colonized in 1895 following its military victory in the Sino-Japanese War. Korea subsequently became part of Japan's burgeoning colonial empire in 1910.

Despite the fact that trade rested rather tenuously on the willingness of Western shipping companies to agree to fair freight rates until Japan had successfully launched its own oceanic shipping enterprises, this arrangement had the added

---

32. Catherine L. Phipps, *Empires on the Waterfront: Japan's Ports and Power, 1858–1899* (Cambridge, MA: Harvard University Press, 2015), 20–21.

33. Karube Tadashi, *Toward the Meiji Revolution: The Search for "Civilization" in Nineteenth-Century Japan,* trans. David Noble (Tokyo: Japan Publishing Industry, 2017).

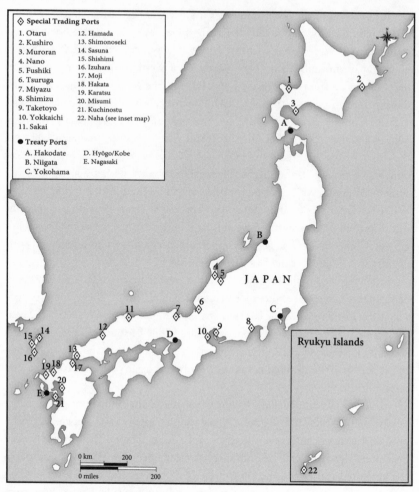

◇ **Special Trading Ports**

1. Otaru
2. Kushiro
3. Muroran
4. Nano
5. Fushiki
6. Tsuruga
7. Miyazu
8. Shimizu
9. Taketoyo
10. Yokkaichi
11. Sakai
12. Hamada
13. Shimonoseki
14. Sasuna
15. Shishimi
16. Izuhara
17. Moji
18. Hakata
19. Karatsu
20. Misumi
21. Kuchinostu
22. Naha (see inset map)

● **Treaty Ports**

A. Hakodate
B. Niigata
C. Yokohama
D. Hyōgo/Kobe
E. Nagasaki

FIGURE 2.5 Japan's Open Treaty Ports, 1899.

benefit of demanding large amounts of Japanese coal to fuel the increased commercial steamship traffic. In fact, half of the special trading ports created before Japan's successful renegotiation of the Ansei Treaties in 1894 (to take effect in 1899) were established for the express purpose of providing coaling stations for commercial and military steamships.

But over time, coal exports made up a smaller share of the coal market, even as extraction increased. By the turn of the twentieth century, domestic coal consumption for industrial production and eventually the production of electricity overtook East Asian export markets and the sale of fuel coal to foreign shipping companies. By the 1920s, Japan was importing more coal than it was exporting to feed its growing military, industrial, and urban sectors. It would soon begin importing oil in mass quantities to fuel its military in the 1940s. So the opening of Japan to global commerce in the 1850s, while certainly beyond the comfort of many Japanese officials that sought tight control over political diplomacy and economic markets, significantly increased the likelihood that Japan would become a major industrial power by the outset of the twentieth century.[34]

In this chapter, we have traced the relationship between politics and carbon energy in the first society to fully industrialize—Britain—as well as the ways in which two subsequent Industrial Revolutions followed or deviated from Britain's model. Coal impacted not just the decisions made by government officials, but also the relationship of ordinary people to work, family, and society. In this sense, we broadened our understanding of politics as not merely something conducted by representatives of governments but as a set of claims and demands that ordinary people made in their daily lives.

Above all, we saw that the shift to coal as the prime mover of industry or as transportation fuel for steamships and railroads was not inevitable. Nor was it always a rational economic decision. Paths both taken and not shaped coal's transformation of economies, social relationships, and international diplomacy. In the nineteenth century and into the twentieth, this process was not confined to the three societies we examined here: Britain, France, and Japan. Other societies industrialized at approximately the same time as France and Japan, including Germany, Belgium, the Netherlands, the United States, and Russia. And beginning in the 1860s, a new fuel—oil—complicated global energy politics even more.

In chapter three we turn to two interrelated developments in the history of carbon energy. As coal came to dominate the energy desires of industrial societies, it reshaped the political landscape. In particular, carbon energy concentrated the political power of workers in ways unforeseen by government officials or the capitalist class. Coal, as some historians have argued, ushered in the age of mass democracy. At the same time, it enabled decidedly undemocratic forms of rule in the places where the raw materials of industry were harvested or extracted. In response to the political power that coal miners and transporters built for themselves, factory and mine owners, in concert with government officials, sought ways to undercut that power. To do so they often turned to oil, the physical properties of which failed in the long run to afford the same kinds of possibilities for political power to those involved in its extraction, transport, and consumption.[35]

---

34. Phipps, *Empires on the Waterfront*, 23, 58–59, 144.

35. Timothy Mitchell, *Carbon Democracy: Political Power in the Age of Oil* (London: Verso, 2013).

FURTHER READING

Allen, Robert C. *The British Industrial Revolution in Global Perspective*. New York: Cambridge University Press, 2009.

Ericson, Steven J. *The Sound of the Whistle: Railroads and the State in Meiji Japan*. Cambridge, MA: Harvard University Press, 1996.

Kirk, Neville. *Labour and Society in Britain and the USA, Vol. 1: Capitalism, Custom and Protest, 1780–1850*. Brookfield, VT: Ashgate, 1994.

Malm, Andreas. *Fossil Capital: The Rise of Steam Power and the Roots of Global Warming*. London: Verso, 2016.

Smil, Vaclav. *Energy and Civilization: A History*. Cambridge, MA: The MIT Press, 2017.

Thompson, E. P. *The Making of the English Working Class*. New York: Vintage, 1966.

3 CARBON DEMOCRACY AND ITS LIMITS

> Coal mining is the most dangerous work in our land today
> With plenty of dirty slaving work and very little pay
> Coal miners, won't you wake up and open your eyes and see
> What this dirty Capitalist system is doing to you and me
>
> —SARA OGAN GUNNING, *"Come All You Coal Miners,"* 1937

In early 1905, regular readers of the *Times* (of London) newspaper would likely have had their attention drawn to coverage of two labor strikes. One broke out in Germany's northwestern coalfields in the Ruhr River valley. On January 15 Theodor Möller, the Minister of Commerce for Prussia (the German Empire's largest state), estimated that the number of striking coal miners had reached 54,000. Möller described the work stoppage as sudden and unexpected. The following day, an assembly of miners' delegates officially declared a general strike. Seven days later, the number had risen to 194,856, or 80 percent of the total number of miners in Westphalia, the province in which the strike erupted.

Echoing the fears of government officials, the *Times'* Berlin correspondent remarked that "a general strike would seriously affect not only the German coal trade, but also the whole industrial life of the country ... large quantities of coal are sent down the Rhine to Holland and up the Rhine as far as Mannheim. Some of the coal is exported by railway to Luxemburg, and even to France. In Hamburg and Bremen Westphalian coal has to contend against supplies imported from England, while in Berlin it encountered the supply from Silesia [mostly located in southeastern Poland]." The strike promised to have dire economic ramifications for one of Europe's industrial juggernauts, particularly in the iron and steel industries, where forging consumed copious amounts of coal.[1]

---

1. "The Strike of German Miners," *Times*, January 17, 1905.

As it turned out, the strike resolved rather quickly. On January 29, Otto Huë, the Socialist Deputy for the city of Bochum (the nucleus of the Westphalian strike's origins), addressed a mass meeting. Huë "declared that in a single fortnight the strike had achieved more than Parliamentary action had achieved in ten years." The strike was itself "an elemental movement of spontaneous origin and growth which derived its strength from unanimity of purpose and from entire absence of party or political colouring."

In other words, Huë assuaged fears among mine owners and government officials that coal miners were merely dupes of international socialism. The miners had practical concerns that transcended ideology. Faced with the real possibility of a protracted labor crisis, the Prussian parliament proposed reforms to address the miners' primary grievances: volatile, depressed rates of pay; regular breaches of the eight-hour workday law; evasion of safety regulations; price manipulation by mine owners; and nonpayment for coal loads that contained impurities.[2]

Huë's pronouncement earned "prolonged cheers" from the workers assembled to learn the latest about the government's response. But they "resolved not to resume work until all their demands had been conceded." Parliament had proposed a bill that favored workers, but it had not yet voted the bill into law. "Come what might," the *Times* commented, "the strike was won and would strengthen the position of the working classes in every branch of industry."

On February 10, the miners' committee recommended a resumption of work, and on March 27, Prussian Minister-President Count von Bülow introduced "the Bill for the reform of the conditions of labour in the mines." Faced with staunch resistance from mine owners, the act ultimately passed was weaker than the proposed bill. But it nevertheless demonstrated the seriousness with which the government addressed the possibility that the country's coal supply lines might soon slow to a trickle.[3] The entire set of events unfolded without any major outbreaks of violence. Readers would likely have concluded that the outcome of the Westphalia coal miners' strike of 1905 represented the very best in government-labor relations.[4]

In stark contrast, the *Times*'s reporting out of the oil fields in the Russian Caucasus offered a more ominous picture. On January 5, 1905, clashes between competing factions within the ranks of naphtha [crude oil] miners at Bibieibat [today Bibi Heybat, Baku, Azerbaijan] descended into violence. One died and ten were wounded. The following day, five died and twenty-six sustained injuries. After

---

2. "The Strike of German Miners," *Times*, January 21, 1905.

3. "The Strike of German Miners," *Times*, January 31, 1905; "The Strike of German Miners," *Times*, February 11, 1905; "Count von Bülow on Social Policy," *Times*, March 28, 1905; *Times*, "The International Congress of Miners," August 12, 1905.

4. For more on the 1905 strike, as well as strikes in 1889 and 1912, see David F. Crew, *Town in the Ruhr: A Social History of Bochum, 1886–1914* (New York: Columbia University Press, 1979), 195–220.

three more days of "fatal labour riots," sixty oil towers had burned to the ground. Over the next month, strikes and clashes spread to other industrial sectors and beyond the epicenter of the strikes in the oil fields on the Caspian Sea coast:

BATUM, Feb. 4: The carmen here have again gone out on strike. Yesterday, 800 workmen forced their way into Samtredi Station and compelled all the officials and telegraphists, under pain of death, to leave it. They then went out to the village of Samtredi and compelled the shopkeepers to shut up their establishments. In a collision with the police that followed a village policeman was killed. Last night the rails were torn up at a place on the line three versts [approximately 2 miles] from Batum ... At Poti all work has stopped in the harbour and no ships are unloading.

TIFLIS, Feb. 4: The strike here continues. The workmen of Bozardschianz tobacco factory and the Tolle Alchanoff soap workers have joined the movement.

VLADIKAVKAS, Feb. 4: In the centre of the town, yesterday, armed robbers forced their way into a shop, while their associates fired off their rifles in the street, wounding four persons who were passing the time. The robbers plundered the shop and escaped. Cossacks [Russian soldiers] have been sent in pursuit.[5]

Reports of labor strikes, violence, and industrial sabotage were not confined to Russia's Caspian oil region. In a reprint of a series of letters from "a Russian lady in St. Petersburg to an English friend," the *Times* conveyed a visceral sense of the revolutionary and counterrevolutionary violence unfolding in late January:

On the Nevsky [St. Petersburg's main street] the soldiers fired on the people. It was awful to hear the savage shrieks and howls of the people ... Heaps of people fell killed and wounded, and it was a confusion of hell. I saw with my own eyes how the mob surrounded the carriage of a much decorated general and asked him to take off his cap. As he refused, one rough struck him in the face with an empty bottle, the bottle broke, and the general's head was one mass of blood. They then fell over him and killed him right out.[6]

What had become by January an outright political revolt against the Russian tsar held its place in the pages of the *Times* for much of the rest of the year. In late February, Tsar Nicholas II conceded the demands of striking rail workers in order to ensure the swift transport of troops to Manchuria, where the Russian Empire

---

5. "The Russian Outbreak," *Times*, February 6, 1905.

6. "The Outbreak in St. Petersburg," *Times*, January 31, 1905.

endured shocking losses at the hands of Japan during the Russo-Japanese War (1904–1905).[7]

Likewise, in late February, a massacre in Baku between the city's Muslims and Christians left at least 2,000 dead over the course of four days. In a letter to the *Times* in early April, British Member of Parliament Henry Lynch offered skepticism over the Russian government's claim that the massacre was a manifestation of deep-seated religious hatred. Lynch, who had travelled in and written extensively about the Caucasus posited that "in the opinion of many local observers, the Russian Government not only took no steps to prevent the massacre, but have come under the suspicion of having connived it."[8]

In September violence erupted again, this time as the tsar's heavily armed Black Hundreds stormed Baku, set fire to oil derricks, and whipped up anti-Armenian sentiment among the city's original Tatar inhabitants, who'd seen the profits from oil flow out of their hands and into the coffers of oligarchic Armenians. That month, the *Times* announced the demise of the Baku oil industry after nine months of revolutionary action: "3,000 out of a total of 3,600 wells are ruined ... The loss is more severe than that caused by a whole year of war."[9]

Carbon Energy and Its Democratic Promise

These two labor conflicts—one in Germany, one in Russia—might have seemed quite different to readers of the *Times*, which tended to emphasize an alleged predisposition for violence among Baku oil workers. But historical perspective affords us a greater chance to unpack the striking similarities that lie beneath the veneer of difference. If we read with a critical eye, what can the ongoing coverage of these two labor conflicts, as reported in the *Times*, tell us about the political role of carbon energy at the turn of the twentieth century?

Westphalian coal miners and Baku oil workers possessed, by the turn of the twentieth century, extraordinary political power within their respective societies. They were not large in number as a percentage of their national populations. But because they handled coal and oil respectively in enormous quantities, their jobs afforded them unique political options.

Miners and derrick operators held the extremely dangerous front lines of sets of highly technical and specialized processes of extracting, loading, and transporting large amounts of carbon energy. The industrial and commercial lives of Germany, Russia, and other industrializing countries increasingly depended on coal and oil. Together with heavers, stokers, pump attendants, locomotive operators, mechanics,

---

7. "The Disorders in the Caucasus," *Times*, February 27, 1905.

8. Henry Lynch, "The Baku Massacre," *Times*, April 1, 1905.

9. "The Anarchy at Baku," *Times*, September 11, 1905; Robert W. Tolf, *The Russian Rockefellers: The Saga of the Nobel Family and the Russian Oil Industry* (Stanford, CA: Stanford University Press, 1976), 150–63.

railyard workers, and stevedores (dockworkers), these coal and oil miners literally kept the lights on and the trains running. Without these flows of energy, industrial life ground to a halt.

Because many of these jobs required either technical expertise or tight synchronization of tasks, those we can call "carbon workers" were not, in the early twentieth century at least, easily replaced. Experience and specialized knowledge mattered. Carbon workers leveraged both for economic and political change.

In short, their jobs as movers of carbon energy afforded them a scale of political power unknown to British textile workers in the 1830s, when manufacturers began the switch from water to coal. While those workers had the ability to stop work at the point of manufacture, mechanization had already devalued their knowledge and experience, rendering workers easily replaceable. And they could not seriously impede the flow of water that powered spinning mules and looms. But by the late nineteenth century, the increased consumption of coal for the purposes of mechanical power throughout much of Europe and North America, along with oil in Russia, meant that those that extracted and transported carbon energy possessed a great deal of political leverage.[10]

It is not a stretch to say that by the early twentieth century, carbon energy and the workers that extracted and transported it had made mass democracy possible, what historian Timothy Mitchell has called "carbon democracy." Carbon workers formed the nucleus of a broader set of demands for the implementation of democratic reforms that extended from coal mines to train depots to dockyards to boiler rooms to shop floors, from city halls to national legislatures to colonial offices.

The power exercised by workers afforded all manner of new political possibilities. For example, following the deaths of nearly 1,100 miners in a Courrières colliery explosion in northern France in early March 1906, surviving miners and their families triggered a general strike among mine, rail, and dock workers that soon spread throughout France. Anarchist (antigovernment) and syndicalist (trade union) leaders developed concrete sets of demands regarding fair pay, safety, hours restrictions, and pensions in the northern coalfields. Over 80,000 coal workers had walked off the job by late March. In 1906 alone, the number of French strikes reached 1309, with 438,466 workers on the picket line at some point during that year. The French employment ministry estimated that over 20 percent of strikers worked in the coal industry alone. The Courrières disaster and the strikes that followed transformed French unions into larger, more formidable, and more radical political organizations than they had been in the years leading up to the explosion.[11]

As Map 3.1 suggests, French miners constituted one sector of a broader mobilization of coal industry workers in industrial societies at the turn of the twentieth

10. Timothy Mitchell, *Carbon Democracy: Political Power in the Age of Oil* (London: Verso, 2013), 19.

11. Robert Neville, "The Courrières Colliery Disaster of 1906," *Journal of Contemporary History* 13, no. 1 (January 1978): 33–52.

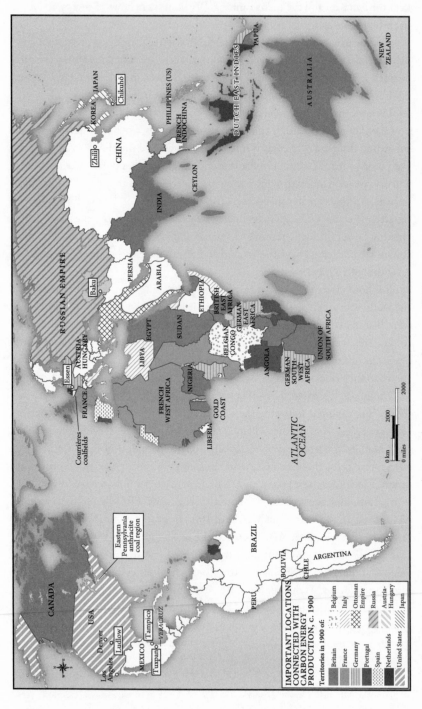

MAP 3.1 Important Locations Connected with Carbon Energy Production, c. 1900

century. From 1891 to 1913, strikes in Britain's mines and quarries combined to produce approximately twice as many workdays lost per employee as textiles, the second most militant industry. Shipbuilding, metal fabrication, and engineering comprised a quarter of the coalfield total from 1891 to 1900 and a fifth from 1900 to 1913.[12] In 1910, concurrent strikes by railwaymen and miners, along with cotton spinners, slowed production for much of the year. In 1911, a national general strike commenced among cleaners, women in the cloth trades, and even British schoolchildren. But the railways, ports, and docks remained at the nucleus of strike activity. That year's railway strike for union recognition followed on the heels of "widespread and often united action on the part of seamen, dockers, carters, tramwaymen, and other workers around the dock areas."

The following year, almost a million British coal workers struck for a minimum wage, which parliament passed five weeks after the strike's commencement. The government did so to ensure that sufficient flows of coal resumed to the factories and electric utilities in London, Manchester, and Glasgow. Coal was also in short supply at Britain's seaport terminals, where Britain's naval and commercial steamships required refueling and where shipping companies exported coal to France and other adjacent European countries.[13]

On the eve of the Great War (1914–1918), intense labor action in Britain's energy sector rocked the birthplace of the world's fossil fuel revolution. The coal that had banished water power, fractured British labor, and consolidated the political power of the capitalist class in the 1840s now threatened to upend the capitalist order that coal had helped make possible.

The power of carbon workers extended from Europe and western Asia to North America. In 1902, the Anthracite Coal Strike Commission gathered testimony from miners and supervisors in eastern Pennsylvania's coalfields. There, militant native-born and immigrant miners had forced the hand of the United Mine Workers of America (UMW) into supporting a strike that lasted five months. By withdrawing their labor at points from which much of the northeastern United States' high-carbon fuel coal originated, miners convinced the national union leadership, headed by John Mitchell, and the coal operators to enter into arbitration over the capriciousness of pay rates, the use of rail cars as measures of a miner's output, and other workplace rules.

The Commission's award, handed down in March 1903, did stabilize and even increase pay rates relative to hours worked for some types of workers, including firemen, pumpmen, and water hoisters. But the Commission refused to force operators to install scales, which likely would have increased trust between miners

---

12. Roy Church, *The History of the British Coal Industry, Vol. 3* (Oxford: Clarendon Press, 1986), 746.

13. Neville Kirk, *Labour and Society in Britain and the USA, Vol. 2* (Brookfield, VT: Ashgate, 1994), 106–07.

and owners. Still, the 1902 strike demonstrated to the UMW that miners' commitments to increased economic security underscored the union's success. The union had "organized the anthracite industry at the turn of the century not so much through its own initiative, but by serving as a vehicle for workers' militancy," historian Perry Blatz notes. By the 1910s and 1920s, the UMW had become one of the most democratically governed and militant labor unions in the United States.[14]

Titans of American oil too had to contend with militant workers. In the small communities south of Los Angeles, the 1920s oil boom generated exorbitant urban growth and wealth accumulation. Oil workers formed the center of growing popular protest against the environmental consequences of unrestrained oil development. In Huntington Beach, local residents—many of whom were directly employed in the oil sector—entered into coalition with fellow homeowners and conservationists. Together, they opposed a 1922 ballot measure backed by real estate developers and the oil industry that would have opened up drilling concessions in Huntington's residential and business districts. The Oil Workers' Union local "hosted a 'general clean up' of the town's vast, oil-polluted beach," which intensified local sympathies to the environmental threats.

The ballot measure failed and the drilling ban remained in place for the rest of the decade. Similar action taken by oil workers in neighboring Redondo Beach squelched an attempt to expand oil production into the city limits. The action ultimately transformed local politics into a competition over which candidates were dedicated to "[public] ownership of water and power, and the regulation of 'offensive' industrial practice."[15] These examples reveal that even outside of the framework of the labor strike, carbon workers could leverage their positions in the energy economy and as powerful local voting blocks in order to limit the kinds of social, economic, and environmental pressures imposed by energy corporations.

The Limits of Carbon Democracy

Despite the increased frequency, intensity, and relative success of sabotage (slowdowns) or strikes, private ownership and government agents dealt out staunch and often violent resistance to carbon workers. Capitalists often called upon local law enforcement to defend their physical assets from sabotage, destruction, or takeover. During a particularly tense set of lockouts over 25 percent wage reductions for some 300,000 coal workers in the British coal districts of Yorkshire, Lancashire, and the Midlands in 1893, a crowd estimated at 3,000 people gathered at Ackton Hall Colliery to prevent the loading of coal by scabs (strike-breakers or replacement workers). The British government dispatched royal troops to reinforce the local

14. Perry K. Blatz, *Democratic Miners: Work and Labor Relations in the Anthracite Coal Industry, 1875–1925* (Albany: State University of New York Press, 1994), 166–67, 229.

15. Nancy Quam-Wickam, "'Cities Sacrificed on the Altar of Oil': Popular Opposition to Oil Development in 1920s Los Angeles," *Environmental History* 3, no. 2 (April 1998): 197–99.

constable, charged with dispersing the crowd on behalf of Ackton Hall's owner. The troops opened fire, killing two miners and injuring twelve.[16]

In Colorado's southern coalfields, extensive networks of company housing, stores, and schools kept many coal workers and their families indebted to the Colorado Fuel and Iron Company (CFI). Paternalistic management practices coupled with mining death rates that reached twice the national average came to a head in September 1913, when fresh Colorado UMW recruits struck. The union funded and organized make-shift open housing beyond the control of the company. The largest tent colony, dubbed White City, was erected at Ludlow (see Figure 3.1). About 1200 striking miners and their families withdrew their

FIGURE 3.1 Striker and children at Ludlow, c. 1913-1914.
Source: Denver Public Library, Western History Photographic Collections.

16. Church, *History of the British Coal Industry*, 736.

labor to White City. If they could hold out long enough, bustling Denver's shrinking coal supplies might force the governor to intervene on their behalf.

As UMW swelled its Colorado ranks in 1913, John D. Rockefeller Jr., who had assumed control of CFI by 1907, attempted to counter the union's appeal. He instituted a 10 percent pay increase, an eight-hour workday, the abolition of script (company store credit that trapped miners in debt), and the provision of unionized checkweighmen to ensure fair payment for coal loads. Rockefeller's self-proclaimed benevolence simply brought CFI in line with Colorado labor law. With decidedly less fanfare and publicity than his announcement of increased living standards for coal miners, Rockefeller hired the Baldwin-Felts Detective Agency, the notorious antiunion mercenary company that had recently machine-gunned striking miners in West Virginia. He had the local sheriff deputize three hundred of them.

Despite intermittent skirmishes and the tense standoff between CFI's agents and UMW, the coalfields remained relatively bloodless in early 1914. But when on the morning of April 20 militiamen demanded that Louis Tikas, the Greek-born strike leader at Ludlow, turn over a captive allegedly held in the camp, tensions spun out of control. Rifle and machine-gun volleys ensued throughout the day. Though the historical record is unclear as to its true origin, White City was ablaze by the afternoon, with dozens of people trapped in the dirt cellars dugout below the burning tents. Four women and eleven children died in the inferno. Militiamen shot Tikas and other organizers in the backs. All told, eighteen miners died in what became known among labor sympathizers as the "Ludlow Massacre."[17] As the American Federation of Labor put it in late 1914, "the militia . . . has acted with the most brutal and wanton license, committing with impunity numerous crimes, from murder of women and children down to petty larceny."[18]

Over the next week, striking miners "dynamited, looted, burned, or otherwise destroyed at least half a dozen mines." By the time the financially strapped UMW gave up the strike in December, sixty-six miners or family members had died in the violence. The federal commission charged with investigating the massacre rejected Rockefeller's suggestion of a company-run union. But the commission's unwillingness to pressure Colorado to bring criminal charges against CFI and its agents intensified suspicions among workers that the government—whether federal or state—often sided with capital over labor.[19]

The war that commenced in Europe in the summer following the violence at Ludlow not only transformed the imperial politics of the leading industrial nations

---

17. Caleb Crane, "There Was Blood: The Ludlow Massacre Revisited," *New Yorker,* January 19, 2009. Also see Thomas Andrews, *Killing for Coal: America's Deadliest Labor War* (Cambridge, MA: Harvard University Press, 2008).

18. *Report of Proceedings of the Thirty-Fourth Annual Convention of the American Federation of Labor* (Washington, DC: Law Reporter Printing Company, 1914), 284.

19. Crane, "There Was Blood."

but their energy politics as well. World War I represented both the triumph of carbon democracy as well as its limits. In Britain and the United States (which entered the war in 1917), the government exempted coal miners, railwaymen, and other industrial workers essential to the war effort from military conscription. The French government banned strikes and assumed the job of setting wages and the terms of working conditions. Similarly, the German state brought the coal industry under the authority of compulsory work councils.

In each of these cases, states intervened directly in the struggle between capital and labor in order to continue their war efforts. They often did so to the chagrin of mine and railroad owners, but in ways that often replaced corporate preferences with state authority. Mitchell has noted that "as workers in industrialised regions fought for a more egalitarian life, the democracy they began to achieve was always liable to slip from providing a means of making effective egalitarian claims to offering a means of regulating populations through the provision of their welfare."[20]

Indeed, Rockefeller and other industrial magnates supported forms of welfare democracy, including Social Security and healthcare. It afforded them effective ways of repressing the demands for what they truly feared: the transfer of profits and ownership from themselves to worker collectives.

Only in Russia, where a second and ultimately successful revolution resulted in the tsar's abdication, did workers achieve such a redistribution of wealth, and only for a short while. Still, as the Allied Powers led by Britain and France imposed the terms of defeat on Germany in 1919, and with the Ottoman, Austro-Hungarian, and Russian imperial orders effectively destroyed, it would be difficult to argue that carbon workers across the industrialized world had not already achieved remarkable levels democratic political transformation through their collective, if sometimes precarious control of energy.

Carbon Empires

Let us now consider the impact of the rise of fossil fuels outside of the regions that both produced and consumed them in large quantities. The emergence of a class of carbon workers that controlled flows of increasingly essential energy afforded those workers greater leverage over their respective political systems than they otherwise would have had. But carbon energy also facilitated the expansion of decidedly undemocratic, imperial forms of political and economic control. Indeed, these processes of empire-building and democracy-building constituted two sides of the same coin.

The point of these imperial projects was not, at least initially in most cases, to find, control, and tap novel stores of coal or oil. Most fossil fuels extracted during this period were consumed relatively close to their geographic origins in Europe,

20. Mitchell, *Carbon Democracy*, 24–25.

Japan, and North America. Rather, the point was, from an economic vantage, to expand the range of raw materials available for manufacturing. Additional agricultural output sustained the growth of industrial workforces reliant on calories to exert energy in factories, in dockyards, and in coal mines, oil fields, and electric power plants in Europe and North America. From the 1870s until the outbreak of World War I, it was no coincidence that the most expansive empires in the world were also host to the leading industrializing societies, which were undergoing dramatic, if contested, democratic transformations.

Dubbed the "New Imperialism" or the "Age of Empire" by historians, this period witnessed the further extension and intensification of European, along with Japanese and American, economic and political dominance. In the decades following Britain's humiliation of China during the Opium Wars (1839–1842 and 1856–1860), where British steam technology proved the critical military difference, a potent mix of fossil fuels, iron, steel, nationalism, scientific racism, and promises of lucrative global "trade" drove a frenzy of colonial expansion. By the 1890s, China's Qing emperor stood essentially powerless in the face of European threats of open colonization unless his government capitulated to unequal trade agreements. Japan too, which had begun rapid industrialization and modernization of its military following the 1868 Meiji revolution, curtailed Chinese influence in Korea, and increased its own, in the First Sino-Japanese War (1894–1895).

In 1878, the industrial powers of Europe claimed only about 10 percent of the African continent. Following European collusion at the Berlin Conference (1884–1885) to substantially increase that proportion, only Ethiopia and Liberia stood as independent African states at the outset of the World War I. Ninety percent of the continent fell under some form of European rule. For example, between 1885 and 1908, Belgium's King Leopold II inaugurated a murderous frenzy of rubber extraction in the so-called Congo Free State to supply Europe's rapidly expanding coal-powered electrical infrastructure.[21]

Likewise, French, British, and German incursions into Southeast Asia brought trade networks and agriculture under European control. In the Pacific and Caribbean, the Spanish-American War of 1898 seemed to turn the United States into an overnight imperial sensation. The United States leveraged its new position as an industrial power to exercise not only direct colonial rule over Puerto Rico, the Philippines, Cuba, and Hawai'i, but also indirect colonial pressure over much of Central and South America. The United States' Pacific empire of islands offered a strategic set of maritime stops at which to deposit large quantities of refueling coal for its increasingly formidable navy. Meanwhile, Japan's burgeoning coal sector, which had rapidly transformed it into an urban, industrial society by the turn of the twentieth century, fueled its imperial rise as well. By 1910, Japan's East Asian

---

21. See Adam Hochschild, *King Leopold's Ghost: A Story of Greed, Terror, and Heroism in Colonial Africa* (Boston: Mariner Books, 1998).

empire included Taiwan, the Ryukyus, South Sakhalin, and Korea, with other parts of mainland East Asia between the two world wars.

What set the New Imperialism apart from the long history of empire-building that had come before it was that it "more completely integrated colonies into an industrial network of extraction, manufacture, and distribution."[22] Carbon energy and industrial technologies were essential to this difference. Let's consider the case of British India. The British East India Company (EIC) received a royal charter in 1600 to conduct seaborne trade from India to Malaya to Japan. But beginning in the late eighteenth century, the EIC conducted itself more like a sovereign power in India. It established a capital at Calcutta, collected taxes, and maintained an army. Company officials involved themselves in organizing and managing the production and export of crops including grain, cotton, and opium. The latter, the EIC used to square its trade imbalance with China.

When Indian subjects rebelled in 1857, the British crown assumed direct authority over the EIC's territorial claims. The Government of India—the official name of the British colonial authority—picked up earlier EIC efforts to build railway lines to connect coastal ports to the agricultural hinterlands, ship goods, transport troops, and ostensibly to prevent famine should the monsoons fail to provide sufficient rainfall for crop production. From 1876 to 1879, drought did in fact engulf India, and the more than 4,770 miles of track already in operation by 1870 carried little famine relief to the colony's agricultural laborers.[23] Millions of Indian peasants starved to death by decade's end, and with more monsoon failures from 1889 to 1891 and again from 1896 to 1902, famine culled more victims. The railroads, totaling nearly 25,000 miles by 1900, again failed to alleviate starvation.

The staggering death toll in India alone—estimates range from 12.2 to 29.3 million (with not less than 31.7 million colonized subjects across Asia, Africa, Oceania, and Latin America)—was not for want of food supplies. In the late 1870s, *New York Herald* journalist John Russell Young revealed the "despotism" of the Government of India, whose policies had already killed 5 million peasants by 1878. The "money which England takes out of India every year is a serious drain upon the country, and is among the causes of its poverty," Young charged. Likewise, British journalist William Digby suspected in 1901 that when "the part played by the British Empire in the nineteenth century is regarded by the historian fifty years hence, the unnecessary deaths of millions of Indians would be its principal and most notorious monument."[24]

---

22. James Carter and Richard Warren, *Forging the Modern World: A History* (New York: Oxford University Press, 2016), 230–31, 240. Also see Heather Streets-Salter and Trevor Getz, *Empires and Colonies in the Modern World* (New York: Oxford University Press, 2015).

23. Tahir Andrabi and Michael Kuehlwein, "Railways and Price Convergence in British India," *Journal of Economic History* 70, no. 2 (Spring 2010), 354.

24. Quoted in Mike Davis, *Late Victorian Holocausts: El Niño Famines and the Making of the Third World* (London: Verso, 2001), 8.

As it turns out, Digby overstated this possibility. Few twentieth-century historians paid much attention to the Indian famines. But at the time Digby, like Young, was hip to the actual causes. British officials claimed that famine was merely the result of prolonged unfortunate weather. But in fact, it was the culmination of the enforcement of "free market" policies by the Government of India combined with the transportation (railroads) and communication (telegraph) technology that ensured the rapid movement of grain and coordination of food prices. Those policies and technologies were simply not intended to alleviate famine but instead to enrich British profiteers.[25]

The plunder of Indian food stores during prolonged drought could not have happened with the speed and devastation that it did without carbon energy. The Government of India offered British steelers and locomotive builders a captive, publicly financed market for railroad construction. Railways developed not to prevent or relieve famine, but to tighten British military control and to export India's agricultural wealth to Europe. Not only were the thousands of miles of tracks laid in colonial India dependent on steady supplies of coal from Britain's mines—the transport cost of which was greatly reduced with the opening of the Suez Canal in 1869—but the grain and cotton extracted from India in the famine years went directly into the mouths of British workers and onto the shop floors of British factories. The cycle of extraction kept going.

Under industrial capitalism, grain fetched a handsomer return in urban Britain and elsewhere in Europe than it did in rural India. When in the late 1890s the monsoons failed for a second time in a generation, peasant farmers living in the regions of India where British officials had ordered the conversion of grain production to cotton experienced the worst of the food shortages. As peacetime famine practically disappeared from Europe, it beset Europe's colonial holdings with such veracity as to inaugurate the infamous "development gap" that continues long after the end of official colonial rule.[26]

In the nineteenth century, the pursuit of empire usually excluded the capture of coal or oil reserves outside of the carbon-based societies in Europe, North America, and Japan. Important exceptions existed though. For example, in the 1880s, German geographer Ferdinand von Richthofen produced geological surveys of Chinese coalfields. In much the same way that British officials in India heralded their efforts and technologies as inherently beneficial to Indians, Richthofen too saw the potential exploitation of Chinese coal as a boon to China. "The opening of the first coal mines is . . . the first step to material and spiritual change of this [Chinese] empire of four hundred million souls. That is how the country is opened

---

25. Davis, *Late Victorian Holocausts*, 26.

26. Davis, *Late Victorian Holocausts*, 9, 15–16, 332; Eric Hobsbawm, *The Age of Empire: 1875–1914* (New York: Pantheon Books, 1987), 29; Sven Beckert, *Empire of Cotton: A Global History* (New York: Vintage, 2014), 337.

to outsiders; they [the outsiders] will quickly expand the working of the mines and introduce European industries, build railroads and telegraphs, and open China to world trade and civilization," he wrote in 1907.

Chinese mines did not ultimately come under direct European control. But Richthofen's surveys nevertheless prompted reform-minded Chinese officials to convince the Qing emperor that he must relentlessly pursue the extraction of natural resources, including coal, lest Europe or Japan forcibly seize China's mineral wealth.[27]

Likewise, in 1908 the British-owned Anglo-Persian Oil Company acquired from the Shah (king) an oil concession in Persia (Iran after 1925). Anglo-Persian promptly sat on it in order to thwart its American, Dutch, and French competitors. But oil proved a different kind of carbon fuel than coal, especially following World War I. Its fluidity and concentration when compared to coal meant that oil could be extracted, transported, and consumed much further afield than coal, which was for the most part consumed relatively close to the initial site of extraction through the first half of the twentieth century.

Moreover, the technological nature of oil's production—derricks not mines, pipelines not railroads, pumping stations not shipping yards—meant that oil companies, rather than oil workers, controlled flows of this increasingly critical energy source.[28] Far more than coal, industrial powers sought to control oil reserves that existed far outside of the urban industrial hubs of Europe and North America, including Latin America and the Middle East. Oil became a critical addition to the slate of labor and raw materials that industrial powers extracted annually from their formal and informal colonial holdings through World War II. The example of Mexican oil sheds light on the limits of carbon democracy.

Oil Violence in Revolutionary Mexico

In January 1921, the officers of the Huasteca Petroleum Company (HPC), the operating subsidiary of the Mexican Petroleum Company, predicted double earnings for the coming year. HPC vice president Herbert G. Wylie announced the operation of twelve new wells. Three more neared completion, and the daily flow of oil through the company's high-capacity pipelines from drilling sites in the Huasteca rainforest to the port of Tampico on the Gulf of Mexico reached 100,000 barrels. "1921 promises to be a banner year in the history of the company," Wylie boasted. He might as well have been speaking of the entire Mexican oil industry, which

27. Ferdinand von Richthofen, *Tagebücher aus China,* ed. E. Tiessen, 2 vols. (Berlin: Dietrich Reimer, 1907), 1: 1, quoted in Shellen Wu, "The Search for Coal in the Age of Empire: Ferdinand von Richthofen's Odyssey in China, 1860–1920," *American Historical Review* 119, no. 2 (April 2014): 339–63.

28. Mitchell, *Carbon Democracy,* 36–40.

reached its peak production at nearly two million barrels in 1921 before declining due to political developments rather than lack of oil.

The brief *New York Times* article that relayed Wylie's brimming confidence also listed the names of officers re-elected. None of them bore Spanish surnames. HPC, like all of the other companies producing oil in Mexico, was foreign owned and managed.[29]

One of the HPC officers re-elected in 1921 was president Edward L. Doheny, who first traveled to the Huasteca rainforest in the state of Veracruz in 1900. Already a successful oilman in southern California, Doheny leveraged his significant wealth and expertise in an emerging Mexican oil market at a time when Mexico's ruling class eagerly courted foreign investment for mining, agriculture, railroad building, and oil drilling (see Figure 3.2).

Doheny struck heavy crude oil at a place called El Ebano in 1901, purchased land near the port of Tuxpan in 1905, and formed HPC as a holding company for that land the same year. By 1910, he was producing steady kerosene supplies for domestic markets in the area that became known as the "Golden Lane" of Mexican oil production. By 1911, HPC was exporting. When the company struck oil at Cerra Azul No. 4 well in 1916, it became the most successful producer in Mexico. It remained in operation until 1938 when the Mexican government, under intense pressure from the country's laboring classes, nationalized the oil industry.[30]

To understand how HPC and other foreign-owned oil companies sustained production in the midst of the Mexican Revolution (1911–1920), let us first briefly examine the political and economic contexts into which these companies waded. HPC's peak production occurred after the commencement of the revolution in 1911. But the roots of big oil's success in the Huasteca lies in a transformative period known as the Porfiriato, named for the military general don Porfirio Díaz, who ruled Mexico from 1876 to 1911. As we will see shortly, the foreign oil companies that arrived during Díaz's reign, continued to extract oil right through the revolution that ended the Díaz government.

During the Porfiriato, a small but highly influential group of advisors called *los científicos* ("the scientists") stressed economic development as essential to national sovereignty, or self-government. Given Mexico's history it is unsurprising that sovereignty was paramount. Mexico won independence from Spain in 1821. But over the next three decades Spain tried to retake Mexico, France invaded, Texas declared its independence, and Mexico lost half its territory to the United States in the Mexican American War (1846–1848). In the 1860s France invaded again.

---

29. "Oil Company Thriving," *New York Times*, January 28, 1921; Myrna Santiago, *The Ecology of Oil: Environment, Labor, and the Mexican Revolution, 1900–1938* (Cambridge: Cambridge University Press, 2006), 363.

30. Jonathan Brown, *Oil and Revolution in Mexico* (Berkeley: University of California Press, 1993), 25–46.

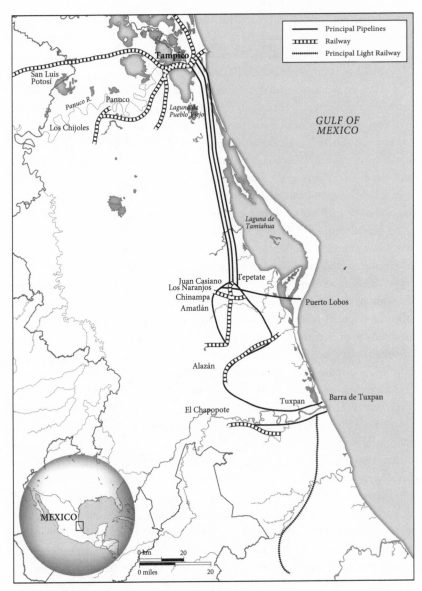

FIGURE 3.2 The Northern Veracruz Oil Zone, c. 1920.

After Mexican resistance drove out Maximilian's 30,000 troops in 1867, North America's Industrial Revolution soon ballooned demand for Latin America's raw materials and agricultural products, including henequen, oil, nitrates, copper, coffee, bananas, sugar, and beef. Díaz emerged, promising to modernize Mexico's economy to increase its sovereignty. Yet paradoxically, Díaz embraced US investment and infrastructure development to increase Mexico's national strength. He championed railroads to link the two countries together and courted American companies equipped with the infrastructure and know-how to survey Mexico's potential for resource exploitation.[31]

We should not be quick to assume that all politics in Mexico either before or after the Mexican Revolution (1911–1920) unfolded as a direct consequence of foreign investment or intervention. Political developments inside Mexico—especially those that preceded the oil boom of the 1910s and 1920s—were critical to the relative success or failure of foreign-owned oil firms.

For example, before the revolution, officials in the Díaz government courted the British engineer Sir Weetman Pearson over the American oil magnates Doheny and Henry Clay Pierce of the St. Louis-based Standard Oil marketing firm Waters Pierce Oil Company. Though Pearson had little oil experience, Díaz preferred his resumé as an engineer. Díaz first partnered with Pearson to construct a canal, a harbor, a railroad, and irrigation works. Likewise, Díaz admired Pearson's polished demeanor and thought Pierce and Doheny rather unlettered and brash. Further, S. Pearson & Sons stood in the good graces of London's foremost financiers. Most importantly, Díaz could use Pearson as a check against the increasingly persistent demands of American oilmen. This lent Díaz plenty of political credibility from a Mexican population wary of American economic plunder, military intervention, land seizure, or all three.

In 1906, the year after Doheny's land purchase near Tuxpan, the Mexican government granted Pearson the largest oil concession to date: "a fifty-year contract covering all national land, lakes, and lagoons in the state of Veracruz."[32] The year after forming La Compañía Mexicana de Petróleo (El Aguila), Pearson's first major successful drilling endeavor at Potrero No. 4 well spewed a crude plume in a one-mile radius over the rainforest.[33] The environmental disaster put El Aguila on the carbon map, and more quickly followed (see Figure 3.3). But the reliable political backing for Pearson's concession all but collapsed with the Díaz regime in 1911.

The role of Huastecan oil in the Mexican Revolution has been a subject of debate among historians. According to Jonathan Brown, as the revolution gained steam in late 1910 and early 1911, little political activity that might have disrupted oil profits visited the Huasteca. Consequently, American and British oil companies were not terribly keen on direct intervention to save the fledgling Díaz regime. Things proceeded relatively well from their perspective. In fact, Standard Oil, no longer satisfied with its indirect involvement and minuscule profits in Mexican oil via its subsidiary, Waters Pierce Co., attempted to secure a more favorable contract

31. Michael Matthews, *The Civilizing Machine: A Cultural History of Mexican Railroads, 1876–1910* (Lincoln: University of Nebraska Press, 2014).

32. Jonathan Brown, "Domestic Politics and Foreign Investment: British Development of Mexican Petroleum, 1889–1911," *Business History Review* 61, no. 3 (Autumn 1987): 388.

33. Brown, *Oil and Revolution in Mexico*, 66–67.

FIGURE 3.3 Oil gusher at Potrero, Mexico, March 15, 1911.
Source: Science and Society Picture Library

with revolutionary opposition leader Francisco Madero. The move drew the ire of the US State Department, wary of charges of American intervention.[34]

But after Díaz fled into exile on May 25, 1911, coincidentally the same day of the first international volume exports of Mexican oil, political violence and democratic revolutionary action soon became central features of the Huasteca oil scene. The regime that had courted foreign oil had fallen, and in its place emerged a dizzying political climate with the potential to radically transform the Huasteca's social, economic, and environmental orders.

Brown's original assessment of the timing of the revolution's impact in the Huasteca has since garnered important revision. As historian Myrna Santiago has revealed, oil workers transformed the tropical coastline into Mexico's foremost hub of revolutionary politics and militant labor organizing on the eve of the revolution, not after it commenced elsewhere. In 1910, oil workers, together with

---

34. Brown, *Oil and Revolution in Mexico*, 96–98.

longshoremen and railroad workers at the Waters Pierce refinery in the port of Tampico supported the opposition candidate Madero.

When federal authorities arrested Madero, who subsequently called for outright revolution, Tampico's working classes rallied in the streets ahead of the November 20 date on which the revolution was to begin. Local authorities promptly arrested the organizers. But after Díaz fled to Paris six months later, a crowd stormed the local jail to liberate the remaining imprisoned Maderistas. The police killed six workers by firing indiscriminately into the crowd. Fighting raged into the night, prompting city officials to call in 150 federal troops and arrest more workers.

In the midst of this political upheaval in 1911, 500 Waters Pierce refinery workers struck for higher wages, an eight-hour workday, overtime pay, and union recognition—similar demands of carbon workers elsewhere in the industrializing world. While not ostensibly a strike with any goals directed at the political outcome of the revolution, the strikers quickly learned how their collective demands intersected with Madero's rather weak hold on power. In response to the strike, Madero dispatched federal troops on behalf of Waters Pierce, betraying his working-class supporters in the oil fields and refineries.

Then in 1912, Madero announced an oil tax. It predictably angered foreign oil companies and prompted the intermittent presence of American and European gunboats on the Pánuco River that flowed from the rainforest's northernmost oil fields to the Gulf of Mexico (see Figure 3.2). Foreign naval destroyers also anchored offshore. Madero's assassination in 1913, which engulfed Mexico in a civil war, only escalated the importance of the Huasteca oil fields to foreign oil, competing revolutionary factions, and workers on the ground. Far from peripheral to the first phase of the revolution, the oil fields, refineries, and shipping terminals were ground zero for radical politics.[35]

As the Mexican Revolution unfolded in the 1910s, the Huasteca rainforest became the site of an intense physical, environmental, and political struggle over the oil economy and the ecological and economic changes it wrought. Pivotal among them was the brazenness with which oil prospectors attempted to strike it rich. For example, when, during the revolution, they could not obtain formal land title from the central government, HPC and others set about doling out large sums of cash to local residents in exchange for survey and drilling leases.

When locals refused to sell outright, companies often resorted to violence. For example, Eufrosina Jacinto and Hilario Flores leased rights to HPC to survey their land at Cerra Azul for 25,000 pesos in 1906. But for four years, few company agents came around. As the lease was set to expire, Doheny offered the family two million pesos for their land in order to fend off competitors. But they refused, now wary of the detrimental health impacts rumored to plague other residents where oil was already flowing.

35. Santiago, *The Ecology of Oil*, 208–11.

Having failed to buy off the family, HPC resorted to more fatal tactics. In June 1911, Otilio López stabbed Jacinto to death. Though he was never caught, residents of Cerra Azul knew López was on HPC's payroll. Jacobo Valdéz, who also worked for HPC, arrived several days later to pressure Jacinto's widow Flores to sell. As he testified in a later case, Valdéz admitted to using "subtle intimidation" to convince Flores to vacate the property.[36]

The assassination of Jacinto cannot be understood simply as an isolated oil-deal-turned-fatal. Jacinto's death occurred amidst the first shots of the Mexican Revolution and at the outset of a steep rise in global oil consumption. Oil had begun to flow in unprecedented quantities along trade routes linking Europe and North America—through their enmeshed networks of railroads, telegraph lines, ports, and canals—to trading partners and far-flung colonies.

Technology and politics served as principle drivers of this acceleration. First, the major navies and commercial shipping companies of the world began to convert their fleets' fuel from coal to oil. Though Mexican crude proved too sulfurous and smoky for the British Royal Navy, US imports of Mexican oil for industrial applications rose dramatically as the more refined American exports found a welcome home in the British war effort. By 1917, American oil comprised 85.2 percent of British consumption, and Mexican petroleum rose from 1 percent to 14 percent of American consumption from 1911 to 1919. The relative ease with which oil could be transported globally coupled with its versatility as a fuel source meant that supplies of oil were easily substituted as demand and consumption rates fluctuated.

Second, the military mobilizations during World War I prompted a steep rise in global oil prices. But just as wartime demand rose, domestic oil exploration in the United States, long the largest producer and consumer of petroleum, entered a brief period of decline. Mexican oil filled the supply gap. Despite the uncertainty of the Mexican political scene, the American and British companies drilling in Mexico reaped enormous profits.[37]

Oil profits, however, came with a cost. Companies often had to pay double taxes to politicians and military commanders, as well as bribes to competing revolutionary armies. As Brown has noted, "No capitalistic organization, least of all these penny-pinching oil competitors, desired to dole out that kind of money to every passing army general and bandit straggler. But the oil companies did just that." Oil was the only successful industry in a Mexican economy ravaged by civil war. Desperate for revenue streams, successive revolutionary governments and their political opponents tapped into oil money in order to finance the revolution. The willingness of oil companies to pay up revealed just how lucrative their ventures had become.[38]

---

36. Santiago, *The Ecology of Oil*, 83–86.

37. Brown, *Oil and Revolution in Mexico*, 104–06.

38. Brown, *Oil and Revolution in Mexico*, 93.

The cost came from below as well. Emboldened by the revolution's rhetoric but skeptical of the intentions of national revolutionary leaders, oil workers disdained the regular racist discrimination doled out by American and British managers. A massive uprising in Tampico in April 1914, which prompted US President Woodrow Wilson to dispatch Marines to protect oil assets, expressed in no uncertain terms the unwillingness of ordinary workers to submit to a global economic order that humiliated them (see Figure 3.4). Even while relative peace visited the Huasteca from December 1914 to 1920 after the Carrancistas revolutionary faction headed by Venustiano Carranza took Tampico, workers continued to frustrate the oil companies. That many workers also fashioned themselves anarcho-syndicalists (anticapitalist, antigovernment, anti-imperialist) meant that they courted repression from the occupying Carrancistas army as well.

Nevertheless, an influx of leftist exiles from Europe and the migration of members of the Mexico City-based Casa del Obrero Mundial (House of the World Worker) to the Huasteca in 1915 offered fresh international socialist and union connections. The newcomers bolstered a rash of worker strikes and, in response, violent state and corporate repression through the end of the revolution. It ended when Álvaro Obregón launched a revolt against Carranza, resulting in the latter's assassination on May 21, 1920. Despite the enormous profits of the war years, Mexican oil production was far from an uncontested frenzy of fossil fuel extraction.

In the long run, foreign oil did prevail over workers, if not the revolutionary state. Though, it was not for lack of effort on the part of workers. The "bust" of 1921 sent shock waves through the oil camps and refineries. Obregón, who became

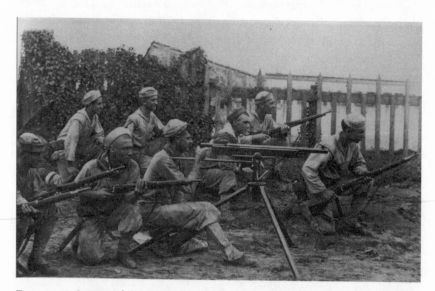

FIGURE 3.4 Men of the *USS Michigan* (BB-27) Battalion on the outskirts of Vera Cruz, c. late April 1914.

Source: Naval Historical Foundation, U.S. Naval History and Heritage Command Photograph. Public Domain.

president after Carranza's assassination, decided to enforce Article 27 of the 1917 constitution. It laid national claim to the subsoil rights for "solid mineral fuels; petroleum, and all hydrocarbons—solid or gaseous."

The principles underpinning Article 27 lay not in anticapitalism but rather in state-managed conservation of natural resources to ensure the long-term material benefit of Mexico's oil. Other state decrees meant taxes on foreign oil companies in the form of land rents and drilling permits. Obregón's government also required that companies pay fines for oil spills. In the minds of these conservationists, foreign companies had extracted oil at such breakneck speed and with such wastefulness that the entire industry was bound to collapse as quickly as it began.

Unsurprisingly, foreign oil executives did not see it this way. The move set the Obregón government on a collision course with these men, who loathed the idea that they might have to compete with the Mexican government, much less each other, for access to Mexico's oil riches.[39] As Frederic R. Kellogg, General Counsel to the Pan American Petroleum and Transport Company begged of his audience at the American Petroleum Institute in New York on November 17, 1920: "If these hopes [that Obregón will cancel regulations] shall be disappointed, is this nation [the United States] willing to abandon those of its children [oil executives] who have tried not merely to advantage themselves, but to advance the prestige and the commercial powers of this nation by developing in a foreign and supposedly friendly country a commodity of which this nation today has need?"[40] While not an open solicitation for US military intervention, Kellogg certainly sought to grease the wheels among his colleagues should a perceived need arise.

Though neither a direct assault on organized labor nor on the principle of privately held property (as Kellogg falsely claimed), Obregón's regulatory intentions nevertheless had the dual consequence of undercutting the political clout of oil workers *and* angering oil companies. In response to Obregón's policies and Article 27, American companies abruptly suspended production, halted exports, and fired somewhere between 10,000 and 25,000 oil workers in mid-1921. Those who kept their jobs saw their wages cut by 20 percent. Obregón dispatched troops to Veracruz under the assumption that the mass layoffs would lead to outright worker sabotage of company property.

Instead, many of those laid off demanded free rail passage to search for work elsewhere. After rains washed out more oil camps in September and the companies fired more workers, Obregón obliged. A mass labor exodus out of the Huasteca oil fields commenced.[41] At that January 1921 board meeting, HPC's

39. Santiago, *The Ecology of Oil*, 216–55.

40. Frederic R. Kellogg, *The World Petroleum Problem: Mexico, Address Delivered before the American Petroleum Institute, November 17, 1920* (New York: Association of Petroleum Producers in Mexico, 1921), 29.

41. Santiago, *The Ecology of Oil*, 251–52.

Herbert Wylie had been correct about the projected health of the company, but only for part of 1921. Though the decline in annual output would not match the 1921 workforce cuts until 1926, by the end of 1921, the executives of HPC and other foreign oil companies operating in the Huasteca began looking elsewhere for the next big oil boom.

Mexico offers a few key lessons. First, it demonstrates that workers possessed critical leverage over flows of carbon energy that forced, at times, negotiations with both oil companies and the state. The corporate exodus of the 1920s certainly did not end the oil industry in Mexico as it were. Several foreign producers hung around until 1938. Strikes in 1924–1925 resulted in the first collectively bargained contract for workers employed by Royal Dutch Shell (today, Shell). The 1928 Calles-Morrow agreement allowed any foreign oil companies that had obtained property prior to 1917 and had performed "positive acts" (produced oil) on that property to retain it. But the onset of a worldwide economic depression in late 1929 combined with floods in 1927 and two destructive hurricanes in 1933 only compounded the declining output. Oil workers grew even more persistent in their demands for improved economic conditions and industry ownership. Add to this, Mexico's domestic industry had become increasingly dependent on oil, which offered the future possibility of a state or even a worker takeover of the industry.

Nationalization, if not collectivization, came to fruition in 1938, in large part because of the persistence and militancy of oil workers. Without such persistence coupled with their ability to slow and at times shut down the flow of oil, these carbon workers would likely not have been able to usher in the fulfillment of the Mexican Revolution twenty-seven years after it commenced. The foreign dominated "colonial economy," as President Lázaro Cárdenas termed it, was to be replaced by one that conserved resources and invested oil profits in Mexico.[42]

But the second lesson proved more fortuitous. Mexico was, in many respects, the first major international oil frontier of the twentieth century. Extraction happened beyond the borders of the nations that consumed the most oil and where the oil companies were based (principally the United States, Britain, and—although it wasn't operating subsidiary companies in Mexico—Russia). But as foreign firms dialed down production amidst worker mobilizations in the 1920s and ultimately lost their stake all together in 1938, the global oil economy proved far more flexible for oil companies than for the coal companies in North America and Europe. New oil frontiers soon emerged, first in Venezuela, where the largest international companies like Jersey Standard and Shell invested heavily amidst the business-friendly policies of President Juan Vicente Gómez.

---

42. Santiago, *The Ecology of Oil*, 326; Brown, "Why Foreign Oil Companies Shifted Their Production from Mexico to Venezuela during the 1920s," *American Historical Review* 90, no. 2 (April 1985): 383.

Perhaps wiser following the rapacious competition that characterized the Huasteca in the 1910s, five American oil companies partnered with Anglo-Persian (Britain), Shell (Britain and Netherlands), and Compagnie Française des Pétroles (France) to form the Iraq Petroleum Company (IPC) in 1928. The cartel's goal was to limit competition for oil concessions throughout the entire Middle East and to secure the most promising ones for themselves.

IPC did not succeed in staving off competition. By 1930, Standard Oil of California (hereafter Socal, today Chevron) had begun to mount a serious challenge to IPC's dominance over Middle East oil. In 1933, Socal inked a deal with King Abd al-Aziz Al Saud (hereafter Ibn Saud) for a vast concession in eastern Arabia.[43] By the onset of World War II, the deal had already begun to radically transform the global politics of carbon energy. Wildly successful in US production but only a minor player in Mexico, Socal initially sought to leverage its Arabian concession to protect its drilling in California. It could simply sit on the Saudi oil fields in order to keep global supply low and prices high, so long as it filled the coffers of Ibn Saud with payments for *not* producing oil. But after the war's end in 1945, Middle East oil supplies offered fresh opportunities to rebuild Europe's ravaged infrastructure and to remake political and economic life.

Oil became the mostly highly circulated global commodity in the second half of the twentieth century. It overtook coal as the primary source of mechanical power and reached 46 percent of total global energy consumption by 1972.[44] Its fluidity and low weight by volume meant that oil could be put to work far afield from its points of extraction. For carbon workers and individual consumers alike, it often meant the erosion of democratic control over essential flows of energy. The nationalization victory of Mexican oil workers in 1938 was one of just a handful of temporary exceptions to this rule.

FURTHER READING

Andrews, Thomas. *Killing for Coal: America's Deadliest Labor War*. Cambridge, MA: Harvard University Press, 2008.

Mitchell, Timothy. *Carbon Democracy: Political Power in the Age of Oil*. London: Verso, 2013.

---

43. Edward Fitzgerald, "The Iraq Petroleum Company, Standard Oil of California, and the Contest for Eastern Arabia, 1930–1933," *International History Review* 13, no. 3 (August 1991): 441–65.

44. David S. Painter, "International Oil and National Security," *Daedalus* 120, no. 4 (Fall 1991): 195; Vaclav Smil, *Energy and Civilization: A History* (Cambridge, MA: The MIT Press, 2017), 274.

Quam-Wickam, Nancy. "'Cities Sacrificed on the Altar of Oil': Popular Opposition to Oil Development in 1920s Los Angeles." *Environmental History* 3, no. 2 (April 1998): 197–99.

Salas, Miguel Tinker. *The Enduring Legacy: Oil, Culture, and Society in Venezuela.* Durham, NC: Duke University Press, 2009.

Santiago, Myrna. *The Ecology of Oil: Environment, Labor, and the Mexican Revolution, 1900–1938.* Cambridge: Cambridge University Press, 2006.

Wu, Shellen. "The Search for Coal in the Age of Empire: Ferdinand von Richthofen's Odyssey in China, 1860–1920." *American Historical Review* 119, no. 2 (April 2014): 339–63.

4 COLD WAR CARBON

Some States appear to hold their breath,
     While others aim to cause the death
Of this "Oil wagon" called a trust,
     Which surely will be hard to bust.
And if it busts I think they'll find
     The same old thing bob up behind.
Yes surely we are in the toil
     Of ever lasting Standard Oil.

—F. L. HILL, *"Standard Oil,"* 1907

In the late 1940s and early 1950s, American movie palace patrons eager to take in the latest Hollywood release likely caught glimpses of newsreels or short informational films before the main attraction. This was not dissimilar from the slew of previews one encounters at the cinema today, but these earlier films were typically created by either the US government or a corporation, not Hollywood studios seeking to generate excitement about forthcoming projects.

One such "short" that postwar moviegoers might have witnessed was a twenty-eight-minute film called *Desert Venture*, which was financed by Standard Oil of California (Socal, today Chevron) and produced in 1948 by renowned industrial photographer Robert Yarnall Richie. As was common then, the film opened with a rolling typed description complemented by uplifting orchestral music:

> This is a story of a venture by American capital in a strange and ancient land . . . A story of the reawakening of a slumbering civilization . . . It has to do with men who went among suspicious strangers and won their friendship . . . Men who challenged heat and sand, and a multitude of obstacles . . . And who won a victory which is serving the interests of the United States, of the country whose resources they are developing, and of a world that moves on wheels. It is the story of oil in Saudi Arabia.[1]

---

1. *Desert Venture*, Robert Yarnall Richie, producer, 1948, https://www.youtube .com/watch?v=4YEtOUWfIuc.

The film offered Socal's version of the first fifteen years of American oil extraction in Arabia, a venture that began in 1933, when Socal and three other American firms jointly challenged the Iraq Petroleum Company's monopoly on Middle East oil by inking a deal with Abd al-Aziz Al Saud (hereafter, Ibn Saud), the debt-ridden monarch of the Kingdom of Saudi Arabia.

Born in 1880 in Central Arabia, Ibn Saud consolidated power over most of the Arabian Peninsula from 1902 to 1932, chiefly by linking his political rule with an ultra-conservative brand of Islam known as Wahhabism. In 1913, on the eve of the Ottoman Empire's collapse during World War I, he captured the oil-rich eastern Ottoman province of al-Hasa on the Persian Gulf. In 1925, with the military support of Wahhab warriors known as Ikhwan, Ibn Saud claimed authority over the Hijaz, the western region home to the Islamic holy cities of Mecca and Medina. Ibn Saud saw this as a boon to his religious credibility, as he could claim to be the protector of the holiest of Muslim places. But his capture of the Hijaz also enabled him to extract taxes from Muslim pilgrims performing the Hajj to Mecca and Medina.

In 1932, Ibn Saud officially declared the unification of the Kingdom of Saudi Arabia. The following year, with the Great Depression shrinking pilgrimage revenues and earlier British support severely wanting, Ibn Saud partnered with Socal (today Chevron), Texaco, Standard Oil of New Jersey, and Socony-Vacuum, the latter two of which later merged to become ExxonMobil. Socal assumed the financial and operational lead in the partnership. The cartel these companies formed, the Arabian American Oil Company (Aramco), became a critical arm of US foreign policy in an increasingly strategic region of the world.[2]

Desert Venture is a relatively forgotten piece of mid-twentieth-century American film. While one can view it in its entirety on YouTube, few, if any, scholars have included it in their analyses. Yet it is remarkable for its insight into the ways in which oil companies hoped to sell their business to consumers after World War II. In this public relations—we might say propaganda—film, Aramco framed its role in Saudi Arabia in three distinct yet interrelated ways.

First, it presented its work in Saudi Arabia as a collective act of bravery, persistence, and triumph on a hostile frontier against oppressive desert heat and leery natives. Aramco's pioneers promised to liberate Arabs from a supposed premodern existence. It was, at its core, a civilizing mission up there with the most expansive imperial ventures in the decades before World War I. As Figure 4.1 demonstrates, by invoking popular representations of nineteenth-century settler expansion across the American West that celebrated victory over harsh environmental conditions and warlike Indians (only in this case, suspicious Arabs), Aramco connected

---

2. Chad Parker, *Making the Desert Modern: Americans, Arabs, and Oil on the Saudi Frontier, 1933–1973* (Amherst: University of Massachusetts Press, 2015), 39–42; James Gelvin, *The Modern Middle East: A History* (New York: Oxford University Press, 2011), 138.

FIGURE 4.1 Aramco's "pioneers" outside the Dhahran mess hall, 1935.
Source: Roy Lebkicher, George Rentz, and Max Steineke, *Aramco Handbook* (Arabian American Oil Company, 1960), 139.

corporate development strategies overseas to one of America's most powerful and enduring twentieth-century national myths: the frontier.[3]

Desert Venture's description of ordinary Arabs fit neatly within this framework. Early on, narrator Dan Donaldson described the Arabian peninsula's inhabitants as essentially "good humored" as they "did a little dance and sang a little song" during the annual wheat harvest—representations that reinforced for Americans the alleged simple-mindedness of those that Aramco was ostensibly there to modernize. Despite this image of the happy-go-lucky Arab, *Desert Venture* also portrayed them as suspicious of Aramco's intentions: shunning handshakes and keeping a watchful eye on American geologists as they surveyed the desert for signs of the oil that lay beneath. Company men had to persist in their efforts to win over ordinary Saudis, which they did through deliveries of goodwill, professionalism, and material benefits.

But *Desert Venture* also folded Arabs into the pioneering image. Arabs worked "side by side with American drillers," were "good students" to their American teachers, and complemented "American technical skill with Arab industry," Aramco argued. "East and West are united in pioneering a new frontier of progress," Donaldson announced. In Aramco's version, Americans and Arabs had become partners in developing Saudi oil. This was not a resource grab, according to the company. Under American tutelage, Arabs could be pioneers in pursuit of their own prosperity.

---

3. On the frontier myth, see, Greg Grandin, *The End of the Myth: From the Frontier to the Border Wall in the Mind of America* (New York: Metropolitan Books, 2019); Richard Slotkin, *Gunfighter Nation: The Myth of the Frontier in Twentieth Century America* (New York: HarperPerennial, 1993).

The second theme was closely connected to the first. *Desert Venture* presented Aramco's business as an act of benevolent intervention and resource development that pulled Saudis out of a supposed state of barbarism, backwardness, and poverty and thrust them into the modern age. According to the film, not only were the American oil engineers, geologists, and their families afforded air-conditioned homes, tennis courts, golf courses, swimming pools, and state-of-the-art medical facilities while in Saudi Arabia. Aramco claimed to raise standards of living of Arabs too. Oil, the company contended, was the "greatest single means to modernize" a country with a "glorious" but nevertheless unforgiving past and usher in a prosperous future. Schools, irrigation, hospitals, and home loans (see Figure 4.2) all stood at the forefront of Aramco's public relations efforts to sell to Americans a story of corporate benevolence. Aramco operated on the belief that "foreign capital cannot justify its presence in a foreign land" without delivering tangible material benefits. Many in the US government concurred.[4]

In this vein, Aramco also cast itself in stark contrast to the brutal European style of colonialism that had recently engulfed the planet in two world wars. In

Figure 4.2 Saudi Arab employee checks with contractor on his Loan Plan home being built in the Dammam area.

---

4. Richie, *Desert Venture*, 1948. On modernization as an American ideology, see Michael Latham, *The Right Kind of Revolution: Modernization, Development, and U.S. Foreign Policy from the Cold War to the Present* (Ithaca, NY: Cornell University Press, 2011).

fact, it was Aramco that probably followed Ibn Saud's lead here, not the other way around. As early as the mid-1930s—before Aramco confirmed large reserves of oil in 1938—the king treated his contract with Aramco as a rejection of European designs on the Arabian Peninsula. After all, the king was quick to point out that he had not accepted either a subordinate role to Aramco or any kind of client relationship with the US State Department. The Aramco concession strengthened rather than weakened the king's ambitions to pursue an expansion of his own political influence in the region, he claimed.[5]

Third, *Desert Venture* promoted oil development as an act of patriotism that, from the perspective of the US government, served America's energy needs and national security. The Saudi venture demonstrated, according to Aramco, the "vitality of the American system of free enterprise," which was supposedly under assault by labor unions and Soviet-led international communism. It was perhaps no coincidence that the year before *Desert Venture* hit theaters, the House Un-American Activities Committee traveled to Hollywood to root out suspected communists working in the film industry.[6] Aramco, in partnering with Ibn Saud, offered a model of global development that countered the state-driven modernization projects of the socialist governments in postwar Europe and Asia, as well as other nationalist development projects, including Mexico's state oil company. It had the potential to deter newly independent states in Africa and Asia, then challenging European colonial rule, from joining a growing international communist movement that opposed US global economic leadership.

This attitude of American government and company officials was simplistic at best and false at worst. The king's direct financial stake in oil profits meant that Arabian oil development was very much state-driven. But more important for the United States' image as the beacon of "free" markets, it was not the *American* but the *Saudi* government that partnered with the oil companies. Aramco would fill the coffers of the Saudi monarch to the tune of 50 percent of profits, which allowed him to generate massive wealth. Since capitalist prosperity was increasingly dependent on large quantities of petroleum, the two pillars on which this alliance was built—carbon energy and material development—only reinforced each other. The Aramco-Saudi partnership would only strengthen over time to the benefit of all involved. Or so company and king asserted.

Near the end of *Desert Venture*, Donaldson turned explicitly to energy itself. Much of the previous twenty-five minutes or so of the film extolled the virtues of the Saudi monarch as a great unifier and of American technological and material progress that brought prosperity to Arabs living on the margins of an ancient desert.

5. Parker, *Making the Desert Modern*, 17–18; Richie, *Desert Venture*, 1948.

6. Steven Mintz and Randy W. Roberts, introduction to *Hollywood's America*, eds. Mintz and Roberts (Malden, MA: Wiley-Blackwell, 2010), 20–22.

But for Aramco, it was important to highlight exactly what made this prosperity and uplift possible: oil, "a truly great contribution to our modern civilization."

As movie patrons settled in for the feature film, they were left with the idea that it was the carbon energy itself that was the main variable in these material and political equations. Without oil, they would not have had the luxury of driving their automobile to the theater to take in the latest feature.[7] Without oil, their American brethren in Saudi Arabia would not continue to enjoy the comforts of suburban life: manicured lawns, air conditioning, and modern hospitals. And the kingdom's Arabs would have remained in a state of supposed backwardness.

Oil's growing importance to international consumerism and national security after World War II did in many respects place Aramco and other international oil giants in positions of tremendous power. Since the companies were often the ones with the readily deployable infrastructure and expertise to get the stuff out of the ground, modern American life depended—or so Aramco claimed—on the ability of oil companies to operate free of government encumbrance. Ibn Saud could not, in other words, have brought about the material changes he claimed to desire for his subjects without Aramco. And ordinary Americans could not live increasingly comfortable, carbon-fueled, middle-class lives without easy access to cheap oil. Indeed, this notion of carbon-based liberation and comfort extended beyond the United States and Saudi Arabia to societies everywhere, including war-torn Europe, where coal was still king. From Aramco's vantage, oil was "keyed perfect to the goal of self support for the nations of the world."[8]

The Cold War and Decolonization

That last quote is critical—the emphasis on "self support" no accident. As Donaldson suggested several times in the film, Aramco was in Saudi Arabia not to tell Arabs what to do but to serve as a partner in resource development. The company presented itself and the United States in stark relief to both the Soviet Union and to the European empires of the twentieth century, including Britain, France, Italy, and Germany. The former, it argued, used coercion to establish communism and unfairly redistribute wealth to the undeserving. The latter, it claimed, also used coercion to hoard wealth that belonged to others.

---

7. The irony is that the automobile and cheap oil helped facilitate American suburbanization, a central feature of which became the in-home television set. With many movie palaces located in major urban areas, fewer Americans took in movies in the late 1940s and 1950s. Far fewer people probably saw *Desert Venture* than might have had oil not fueled this transformation of American living. See Mintz and Roberts, introduction to *Hollywood's America*, ed. Mintz and Roberts, 20.

8. Richie, *Desert Venture*, 1948.

This was both the start of the Cold War and the start of what came to be called decolonization—the formal end of European imperialism. And no matter the local context, both of these global transformations demonstrated just how central carbon energy had become to preserving peace, waging war, and at once maintaining and challenging systems of political and economic power. Aramco was but one corporate player in a game that also involved government officials, carbon workers, and energy consumers.

In chapter 3, we saw how the rise of coal in industrializing nations presented new opportunities for ordinary people to chart democratic courses in their workplaces and societies. We also saw that oil offered similar possibilities in Russia, the United States, and Mexico in the early twentieth century. But because of its unique physical properties that allowed it to become the world's first truly global fossil fuel, by mid-century, oil presented workers with sets of challenges that did not exist in the coalfields of Germany or Britain. It became more difficult for workers—and easier for companies—to control international flows of oil. The relative ease and cheapness of extraction and transport when compared to coal made oil a far more global commodity.

Consequently, oil began to threaten the European and North American democratic orders that had been built on coal. It also undermined the possibilities for broad-based forms of democracy in countries seeking liberation from foreign domination.[9] But we cannot understand how oil did so without first understanding the growing international importance of oil during World War II and subsequently the political and historical contexts of the Cold War and decolonization that followed the war's conclusion.

Mexico's oil nationalization in 1938 spelled potential disaster for Britain on the eve of World War II. Not only could Mexico withhold critical oil supplies at a time when the world lurched toward another global conflict, the Mexican government responded to a boycott by the major American and British oil companies by selling oil to their rivals: imperial Japan and Nazi Germany. Both countries lacked sufficient domestic supplies of oil for transport trucks, aircraft, and naval ships. In 1939, for example, Japan imported 80 percent of its oil from the United States with nearly all of the remaining 20 percent coming from the Netherlands East Indies (which later became Indonesia), where Royal-Dutch Shell and two American companies controlled the oil fields, pipelines, and refineries.

Nazi Germany too remained dependent on foreign oil. Hitler's military began to purchase oil from the Soviet Union in the summer of 1939 and allied with oil-producing Rumania (today spelled Romania) in November 1940. These calculations were hardly formulas for energy security in wartime against relatively

---

9. Timothy Mitchell, *Carbon Democracy: Political Power in the Age of Oil* (London: Verso, 2013), 5–11.

energy-secure countries like the United States and USSR. Nazi commanders clearly recognized this imbalance. In 1942 they marched east to cutoff the Soviet Army from the Baku oil fields. The American bombing of German oil terminals further crippled the Axis war effort in Europe.

Mexican oil had the potential to offer Japan and Germany a way out of this energy cul-de-sac on the eve of Japan's attack on Pearl Harbor and on the American fleet stationed in the Philippines in December 1941. But already aware of the implications by November of that year, the US government intervened in Venezuela to prevent a similar deal from materializing. American officials helped negotiate a 50–50 profit-sharing agreement between the Venezuelan government and the US and British/Dutch firms that operated Venezuela's oil fields in order to ensure an abundant supply for the war effort. The agreement effectively cut Japan and Germany off from Venezuelan oil. A subsequent agreement with Mexico undermined German and Japanese access there. Consequently, the Axis powers suffered chronic fuel shortages throughout the war.

Now relatively flush with oil, albeit from foreign sources, the British Royal Navy could maintain control of Atlantic and Indian Ocean sea-lanes and defend Britain's colonies in the Middle East from German and Italian incursion. By war's end, control over the world's oil supply had become central to maintaining dominance in global politics. It is no coincidence that the two main protagonists of the Cold War—the United States and Soviet Union—emerged from World War II relatively secure in their domestic oil supplies.[10]

The Cold War, which dominated global politics from 1945 to 1991, constituted one side of the politics of carbon energy after World War II. Though allies in the fight against German and Italian fascism from December 1941 to the end of the war, the United States and Soviet Union emerged victorious in 1945 but suspicious of each other's intentions. Would the rebuilding of war-torn Europe mean the expansion of American-style capitalism and representative democracy? Or would it mean the advance of Soviet-style communism that by the 1940s featured repression of dissent, secret police, famine, and one-party totalitarian rule led by Josef Stalin—a far cry from the socialist utopia envisioned by the Bolsheviks in 1917?[11]

This dichotomy, frequently presented by American officials, was of course a false one. Capitalist societies can be totalitarian as much as communist societies can be democratic. Moreover, few societies in history have been wholly capitalist or communist. For instance, after the Russian civil war of 1917–1921, Vladimir Lenin

---

10. Painter, "International Oil and National Security," 188–90; Daniel Yergin, *The Prize: The Epic Quest for Oil, Money, and Power* (New York: Simon & Schuster, 1991), 305–88; Rashid Khalidi, *Sowing Crisis: The Cold War and American Dominance in the Middle East* (Boston: Beacon, 2009), 45–46.

11. For an overview of the Cold War, see John Lewis Gaddis, *The Cold War: A New History* (New York: Penguin, 2005).

implemented a "New Economic Policy" that supported private enterprise in farming and small-scale manufacturing alongside state-owned banking, transportation, steel-making, and oil production.[12] Similarly, during World War II, US President Franklin Roosevelt proposed a state-owned oil company to take over the Middle East concession rights of the privately-held American companies in Saudi Arabia and Iraq. Likewise, the British government, which owned a controlling share of Anglo-Iranian Oil Company since 1913, by 1947 had nationalized, albeit temporarily, its own coal, steel, and railway industries.[13]

But for many Americans, from politicians to business magnates to ordinary consumers, the choice was clear-cut. Only US leadership should fill the void left open at war's end. Stalin's advances in eastern Europe during and after the war portended disaster. To counter the Soviets, the US government and its corporate allies decided to inject massive sums of capital into infrastructure projects: railways, highways, skyscrapers, power plants, and other features of modern urban life destroyed by aerial bombardment and artillery fire. Corporate-led development was to be the antidote to the supposedly infectious spread of socialism, then gaining popularity throughout much of postwar Europe and in Europe's colonial empires. CEOs, including those at America's largest oil firms, sought to beat back international communism with vacuum cleaners and V8 engines rather than battalions and bombs.[14]

A critical irony to the supposed inherent opposition between capitalism and communism was that both relied on copious amounts of carbon energy and natural resource extraction. Rigid adherents to both ideologies saw nature as a resource to be used by humans, a similarity that is often forgotten in the rush to contrast.

Decolonization, in tandem with the Cold War, constituted the second major political development that shaped and was shaped by the pursuit of carbon energy after World War II. As the American rebuilding project in Europe picked up pace in the late 1940s and 1950s under the auspices of the European Recovery Program (popularly called the Marshall Plan), developments in Britain's and France's vast colonial empires in Asia and Africa presented American officials with another conundrum. If the United States was to be a global economic and political leader and extend its stated value of freedom across the globe, it would need to help facilitate the end of its allies' empires. At the same time, it would also need to assume a supportive role in bringing material prosperity to colonized people challenging European imperialism. From the American perspective, its active support—as evidenced by the dizzying number of pacts and treaties to which it became party (see Map 4.1)—was entirely necessary to fight off what US officials characterized

---

12. Stephen Cohen, *Soviet Fates and Lost Alternatives: From Stalinism to the New Cold War* (New York: Columbia University Press, 2009), 2.

13. Painter, "International Oil and Energy Security," 192.

14. See Victoria de Grazia, *Irresistible Empire: America's Advance Through 20th-Century Europe* (Cambridge, MA: Harvard University Press, 2005).

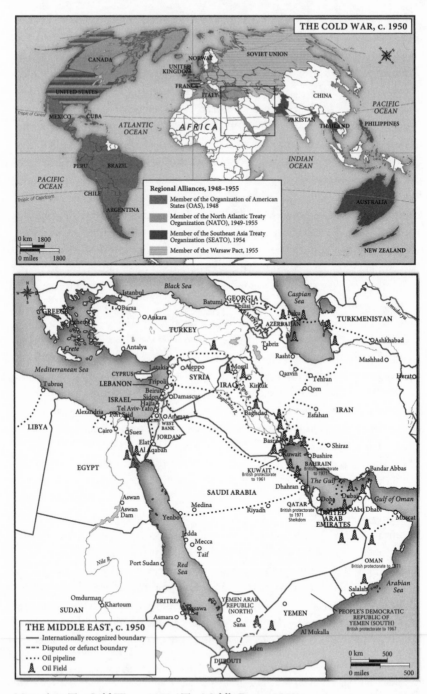

MAP 4.1 The Cold War, c. 1950 / The Middle East, c. 1950

as an aggressive Soviet-led communist takeover. The era of decolonization, which most often refers to the period between 1945 and 1965 and to the end of formal European colonial rule, presented both challenges and opportunities to the US government and to those companies that often shared its interests, including the oil companies.

After some initial victories in the late 1940s that brought to power national liberation governments in Syria (1946, from France), India and Pakistan (1947, from Britain), and Indonesia (1949, from the Netherlands), a cascade of anticolonial actions—some peaceful, some violent, some both—swept the colonized world. Britain and France, together with Belgium, Portugal, and the white settler Union of South Africa, tried to ward off the collapse of their imperial projects. But empty promises of greater autonomy or modest reforms could not contain the momentum of these popular movements. As France's 1954 military defeat at Dien Bien Phu, Vietnam attests, European efforts to maintain their empires were dwarfed by the popular actions from below and the increasingly anticolonial stance of the newly created United Nations. Between 1959 and 1963, thirty new states emerged from colonial domination. More followed suit in the late 1960s and 1970s.[15]

Despite the fact that I just discussed the Cold War and decolonization as separate developments, they intersected at virtually every moment and in every place. For example, as early as 1945, Harry Truman's administration saw a prosperous France as paramount to a US-led global economic and military order—a postwar stability that US officials and French Président Charles de Gaulle believed was threatened by the French Communist Party. At the same time, French officials, including de Gaulle, desperately wanted to revive control of their Vietnamese colony in Southeast Asia, which Japan had occupied for five months before its formal surrender to the United States on September 2, 1945. That same day, Ho Chi Minh, leader of the Communist Party of Vietnam and acclaimed nationalist hero, declared Vietnam's national independence from France. In no uncertain terms, de Gaulle conveyed to US State Department officials how the two were linked: "If the [French] public here comes to realize that you [the United States] are against us in Indochina [Vietnam], there will be terrific disappointment and nobody knows to what that will lead. We do not want to become Communist; we do not want to fall into the Russian orbit, but I hope you will not push us into it."[16] De Gaulle's veiled threat is instructive here: he would rather ally with French communists and risk alienating his American allies, if it meant halting decolonization.

In order to understand the links between the Cold War and decolonization, it is also critical to understand that since the end of World War I, leaders in both

---

15. Todd Shepard, introduction to *Voices of Decolonization*, ed. Todd Shepard (Boston: Bedford/St. Martins, 2015), 10.

16. Quoted in Marilyn B. Young, *The Vietnam Wars, 1945–1990* (New York: HarperPerennial, 1991), 22.

the USSR and United States had positioned themselves as sympathizers with anticolonial nationalists around the world. But each side defined freedom from colonial domination in often oppositional terms. For example, in 1920, Vladimir Lenin concluded that "capitalism has grown into a world system of colonial repression and financial strangulation of the overwhelming majority of the people of the world by a handful of 'advanced' countries."[17] Given Lenin's steadfast critique of capitalism, it is unsurprising that he lent Soviet support to the calls for decolonization emanating from Britain's and France's holdings in Africa and Asia.

Conversely, in 1918, American president Woodrow Wilson called simultaneously for "the removal, so far as possible, of all economic barriers and the establishment of an equality of trade conditions among all the nations" and "a general association of nations . . . for the purpose of affording mutual guarantees of political independence and territorial integrity to great and small states alike."[18] Though Wilson, unlike Lenin, did not specifically call for the end of British and French colonialism (or American colonialism for that matter), he nevertheless defined a set of international aspirations to which colonized people would increasingly try to hold the United States to account. Following Nazi Germany's defeat in 1945 and indeed as early as the Paris Peace Conference in 1919 that formally ended World War I, politicians on both sides of the eventual Cold War divide struggled to match their anticolonial rhetoric with substantive action.

Energy Recovery

With some understanding of how the Cold War and decolonization intertwined, we are positioned to see how both intersected with the politics of carbon energy. While US officials primarily focused their recovery efforts on Europe, they turned to the oil companies operating in the Middle East for assistance. In other words, the rebuilding of Europe was to involve energy connections to the former Ottoman territories that Britain and France had ruled as League of Nations Mandates between the two world wars. And why not? As *Desert Venture* illustrated for viewers, the global rather than regional distribution of oil promised to ensure steady supplies of energy to virtually anywhere.

From Aramco's vantage point, as well as from that of Iraq Petroleum Company and Anglo-Iranian Oil Company (today, BP) then operating in Iran, no region of the world was more in need of a reliable dose of oil than postwar Europe. After all, the US government, eager to keep the domestic economic recovery going after

---

17. V. I. Lenin, *Imperialism: The Highest Stage of Capitalism* (New York: International Publishers, 1939 [1920, 1917]), 10–11.

18. Woodrow Wilson's Fourteen Points, Articles III and XIV, January 8, 1918, *The Avalon Project: Documents in Law, History, and Diplomacy*, http://avalon.law.yale.edu/20th_century/wilson14.asp.

the war, imposed strict import quotas that prevented the companies that ran these carbon cartels from flooding the American market with cheap Middle East oil (it's unlikely that they would have anyway, as it would have threatened profits). Plus, there were no vast oil fields in Europe except within the Soviet sphere to the east. Further, Europe's coal mines lay in disrepair following the war. Acute fuel shortages in the late 1940s demonstrated just how dependent Europeans had become on coal.

At this point, it might be easy enough to see why American investment, in the absence of sufficient European capital, was necessary to a successful European economic recovery. But why oil? What did it matter if Europeans could now gain steady access to Middle East oil? Why not rebuild Western Europe's devastated coal industries laid to waste by massive bombing campaigns?

There are three main answers to this question. First, from the perspective of oil companies, the switch to oil was cheaper. The flow of Saudi, Iraqi, and Iranian oil to Europe after 1945 helped in the recovery effort and alleviated the need to ship American, Bolivian, and Venezuelan oil across the Atlantic Ocean at a time when consumer demand in the Western Hemisphere was on the rise and US domestic production was in decline. As US war planners noted as early as 1943, US production could barely keep pace with increased domestic and international appetites.

That year, members of the Roosevelt administration proposed an International Petroleum Commission tasked with managing oil production and distribution. The commission was to prevent the governments of Iraq, Iran, Saudi Arabia, Kuwait, and others from asserting national control over oil supplies (as Mexico had in 1938)—thus depriving European partners of the cheapest possible oil payments. But the international oil companies saw the commission as a government attempt to dictate where, when, and how much oil they should produce. Few oil executives were interested in increasing supply, which would only decrease their profits. In the face of intense opposition from US oil executives, the commission never materialized.[19]

The second reason for Europe's post-1945 transition from coal to oil was that despite constant claims of shortage from government and corporate representatives alike, oil stood as the most widely circulated global commodity by 1945. Moreover, near the end of the war, American planners and their European partners sought to shore up and stabilize the global capitalist market lest the risky monopolistic practices of the early twentieth century produce another global depression. At Bretton Woods, New Hampshire in 1944, planners organized the International Monetary Fund (IMF) and the International Bank for Reconstruction and Development (today, the World Bank). They pegged the US dollar to gold at $35 per ounce in order to stabilize international currency markets. Those governments that signed

---

19. Painter, "International Oil and National Security," 191; Mitchell, *Carbon Democracy*, 117–18; Yergin, *The Prize*, 547–48.

on to this "Bretton Woods system," as it has come to be known, agreed that the US dollar would serve as the basis of international exchange. Other countries tied the value of their own currencies to the value of the dollar.

In reality, however, it was not the gold standard but instead the fact that the nations of the world now had to buy raw materials (including oil) with US currency that propped up the value of that dollar from the mid-1940s through the late 1960s. Oil transactions, completed using dollars, became critical to the revitalization of Europe. As early as 1947, over half of Western Europe's oil came as purchases from US oil companies, using US dollars. As American oil companies ramped up production in the Middle East, in part to compete with their British counterparts, the flow of dollars to these companies as payments for barrels of crude established the Middle East as a vitally strategic region for Europe's energy security. The absence of an international commission to control and regulate oil production and distribution assured the oil companies immense power within this system, including the ability, when opportunities arose, to influence local political circumstances in producer countries.[20]

The third reason for the switch from coal to oil had to do with the balance of power in those carbon democracies born in the early twentieth century. By controlling the supply of Middle East oil to Europe, oil companies, along with Western governments, hoped to constrain and manage rather than enhance or support the power of workers to affect political change. In particular, they took aim at the coal unions, which had, as we have seen, built up formidable challenges and alternatives to monopoly capitalism by the 1920s. British lawmakers took the lead in 1947 by nationalizing the country's coal industry less than ten years after they castigated Mexican officials for doing the same with oil in 1938.

On the European mainland, the centerpiece of this joint corporate-state challenge to organized labor was the European Coal and Steel Community (ECSC). Established in 1950 on the initiative of French and German coal and steel companies and their postwar government allies, the ECSC established price controls and production quotas. These measures ensured a more stable availability of coal and steel. They also served to undercut the more radical demands of unionized workers for collective ownership. According to ECSC's member companies, their control of carbon energy, rather than the collective control of workers, served vital economic and security interests. American officials agreed and supported the mechanization and integration of French and German coal to reduce workers' political leverage.[21]

The switch from coal to oil not only undercut European broad-based democracy represented primarily by strong labor unions (as we saw in chapter 3), but also

20. Mitchell, *Carbon Democracy*, 111; David Painter, "Oil and the Marshall Plan," *Business History Review* 58, no. 3 (Autumn, 1984): 361.

21. Mitchell, *Carbon Democracy*, 29; John Gillingham, *Coal, Steel, and the Rebirth of Europe, 1945–1955: The Germans and French from Ruhr Conflict to Economic Community* (Cambridge: Cambridge University Press, 1991).

in Middle East producer countries. By establishing oil concession partnerships with undemocratic rulers, including the monarchs Amir Faisal (Iraq), Ibn Saud (Saudi Arabia), and Reza Shah (Iran), Western oil companies hoped to insulate themselves from the demands of workers in the oil fields. Beholden to the development dollars paid by IPC, Aramco, and AIOC respectively, these authoritarian rulers took direct, sometimes violent action, to prevent popular participation in governance.

Middle East oil, controlled primarily by American and British petroleum companies at least until the 1960s (with few interruptions), served as a key weapon not only in the Cold War confrontation with communism in Europe that government officials and CEOs claimed—often falsely—reverberated from union halls, steel mills, and coal mines. Oil also guarded against calls to share resources and wealth with former colonial subjects. American and British government officials considered the oil partnerships with Middle East authoritarians as critical to deflecting Soviet influence in what came to be known during the Cold War as the "Third World," the nonaligned or yet-to-be-aligned countries then emerging from colonial rule.

Oil and Democracy in the Middle East

Prior to the Cold War, the largest British, Dutch, French, and American oil companies held concessions, or contracts, for the Middle East's three largest oil fields in Iraq, Iran, and Saudi Arabia. All three concessions emerged before World War II through partnerships with monarchs that had mostly been installed by Western powers after World War I. These monarchs were eager to expand their own influence in the region.

But the initial goal of the companies was not to pump endless supplies of Middle East oil. Instead they hoped to suppress and manage the region's oil development in order to maintain the illusion of chronic global shortage and thus higher market prices. In the case of the Saudis, Aramco paid Ibn Saud for not insisting that the company produce more oil, and then negotiated tax breaks with the US Treasury to recapture the lost revenue.

But as oil became critical to the European postwar economic recovery, the line that Aramco's parent companies previously offered for keeping their drilling rigs idle now rang hollow (see Figure 4.3). Moreover, the United States' strategic interest in the Middle East evolved rather dramatically in the first two decades of the Cold War. As Britain and France relinquished the colonial authority in the Middle East that they had exercised under the League of Nations Permanent Mandates Commission between 1920 and 1945, the United States stepped in to fill the power vacuum lest its Cold War rival do so.

The power politics of the Cold War though was not simply confined to the corporate board rooms of the oil giants, the White House, or the Kremlin. Ordinary Arabs, Persians, Kurds, and others—along with the elites in their respective societies—shaped the quest to control the region's oil. This intersection of Cold

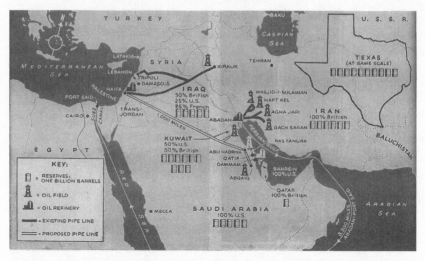

FIGURE 4.3 Middle East Oil: trouble erupts as great powers jockey for the power that petroleum provides.
Source: Life, 11 June 1945.

War politics and local aspirations for self-determination often pitted foreign oil companies against their own governments, nationalist governments in the Middle East, and ordinary people challenging foreign domination over their natural resources and political autonomy.

Iran constitutes the first major site of political contestation over oil in the postwar Middle East. Prior to World War II, Iran was the only country in the region in which British oil interests held exclusive rights. During World War II, both Britain and the Soviet Union occupied Iran in order to secure military supply routes. Reza Shah Pahlavi, who had come to power in 1925, resisted the occupation. But he ultimately abdicated his throne in 1941 under popular pressure from the Iranian working class: political demands from below that both the British and Soviets supported upon their invasion of Iran. When the Shah's son Mohammad Reza Pahlavi (hereafter, Reza Shah) came to power that same year with British help, he negotiated an extension of the British-Soviet occupation until six months after the war's conclusion, whenever that might be.

The ink on the peace treaties was barely dry before Iran's oil fields became ground zero in the standoff between the United States and USSR. American policymakers increasingly regarded Iran as a strategic buffer zone between its Soviet ally-turned-adversary and US oil interests in Saudi Arabia and Iraq. The US postwar position on Iran reflected the emergence of what later became known as the domino theory of Soviet aggression. Iran was an early testing ground for the US assumption that should one country ally with the Soviet Union, neighboring countries would too. Before one knew it, communism would dominate the world. In the Middle East, Soviet control would deprive Western Europe of vital supplies of carbon energy.

While on paper a defensive posture, the domino theory entailed aggressive political and economic maneuvering. American oil executives and US government officials alike began to seek greater control of Iranian oil. In 1945, American oil prospectors began operating near the Soviet border, a clear affront to Soviet influence as well as to the British-controlled Anglo-Iranian Oil Company. Soviet officials too hoped to secure an oil concession in northern Iran as a condition of their withdrawal after the war. Soviet Premier Josef Stalin backed a separatist movement of ethnic Azeris living in northern Iran in order to bring those oil fields firmly within the Soviet orbit. Something had to give.

But both the Americans and Soviets ran into a spate of political obstacles on the ground in their attempts to tap Iran's carbon energy potential. First, Iranian oil workers organized a powerful series of strikes in the oil fields and refineries in 1945–1946. They demanded raises, safer conditions, and an end to the racial discrimination that characterized AIOC's operations, including in company housing. The radicalism of the oil workers proved potentially detrimental to both US and Soviet attempts to secure control over at least a portion of Iran's oil production.

A second obstacle emerged in 1947 when Iran's legislature, the Majlis, passed a law prohibiting any future oil concessions to foreign companies. Lawmakers also required the government to secure a better agreement with AIOC. Future Prime Minister Mohammed Mossadeq, once quoted as saying "the source of all the misfortunes of this tortured nation is only the [British-owned] oil company," led the charge. Mossadeq's loose but vocal coalition known as the National Front pushed for oil nationalization. The Front's longer-term goals of democratic parliamentary reforms, including the ouster of the Shah from politics, were to come only once Iran's oil economy was liberated from British domination.

Mossadeq assumed the prime ministership upon overwhelming parliamentary support on April 28, 1951. Three days later, the Majlis voted to nationalize AIOC's assets, abruptly cancelling the company's oil concession originally set to end in 1993. As a result, Mossadeq's tenure as PM was to last a little over two years.[22]

Given the amount of opposition to nationalization coming at Mossadeq from all angles, it is a wonder that it ever succeeded at all. Clearly Britain opposed nationalization. Iran's oilfields constituted 76 percent of AIOC's production. The rest primarily came from neighboring Iraq. The removal of that much oil from its balance sheets would spell disaster. At best, AIOC would be reduced to a mere transporter and marketer of Iranian oil to Western Europe. Power would soon swing to the American-controlled fields in Saudi Arabia, British officials lamented.

But the Soviet Union also opposed nationalization, not simply because the state-owned Soviet oil company had designs on Iran's northern oil fields. Iran's

---

22. Mary Ann Heiss, *Empire and Nationhood: The United States, Great Britain, and Iranian Oil, 1950–1954* (New York: Columbia University Press, 1997), 5–13, 17–18; Mitchell, *Carbon Democracy*, 107; Mossadeq quoted in Yergin, *The Prize*, 455.

Tudeh (Communist) Party—the Soviet Union's key on-the-ground ally in Iran—also bitterly rejected oil nationalization. The Tudeh enjoyed widespread support, especially from oil workers still reeling from the state crackdowns on their labor organizing in 1946. Mossadeq and the National Front he represented were no friends of organized labor and some Front members were virulently anticommunist. From the Tudeh's perspective, nationalization simply meant replacing corporate domination with state domination. They wanted neither.

On the other end of the political spectrum, Iran's conservative monied interests, including Reza Shah, rejected nationalization given that many of them had grown rich through partnerships with AIOC. They saw no reason to eliminate the primary source of their fabulous wealth. Mossadeq and his allies were certainly up against powerful forces both internal and external, popular and elitist.

In 1951, Britain's Foreign Office began to rally international oil firms to an economic embargo against Iran in order to bring Mossadeq to heel. American firms, relatively fresh off the Mexican appropriation of 1938 (see chapter 3), were more than willing to comply. In any case, declining production in Iran, where they had no real financial stake, meant lower global supply and thus higher prices. Initially, Mossadeq enjoyed the benefit of a hands-off approach from the US administration of Harry Truman. Though mostly sympathetic to the British position in the Middle East, several of Truman's cabinet officials were also loath to defend the interests of "big oil." Too many antitrust battles in the preceding years had garnered the largest oil companies few allies in Truman's Justice Department.

Moreover, Truman's international outlook was in 1952 still motivated by what historian Rashid Khalidi has called "residual anticolonial impulses and . . . a vague sympathy with anticolonial nationalism in the third world." So, despite the fact that Mossadeq was scrambling to keep his country's oil industry producing sufficient quantities for global export and to find willing buyers, in mid-to-late 1952, nationalization stood a fighting chance.[23]

The situation shifted in November, when Americans elected Dwight Eisenhower. The incoming Republican administration brought with it in early 1953 a much friendlier posture toward large corporations, including oil companies. Eisenhower also towed a much harder line against any form of anticolonial nationalism that featured state expropriation of private assets. To do so though, Eisenhower had to conveniently overlook the fact that the British government, America's closest ally, held a controlling share in AIOC, making it a state-owned company as well.

If Truman's Secretary of State Dean Acheson (s. 1949–1953) had actively supported Mossadeq with offers of economic and technical assistance,

---

23. Khalidi, *Sowing Crisis*, 171.

Eisenhower's Secretary of State John Foster Dulles (s. 1953–1959), a former banker cozy with international oil, was eager to undermine those efforts. Compare the position of each of these officials in US state department cables issued just four months apart:

> The Iranian situation continues to deteriorate at an accelerated pace. We are faced with three choices: First, to take no action in the hope that the Iranians will become more amenable [to a US solution] as their internal situation worsens. Second, to support the [Mossadeq] government by providing very large scale budgetary aide. Third, to find a solution to the oil problem and provide funds incident thereto which will bolster up their economy until they can derive substantial income from the flow of oil. For a long time we have felt that the first, in light of their precarious internal situation, was far too dangerous for us to consider. This has been the [British] policy and it has been tried unsuccessfully for 20 months.
>
> —Memorandum by the Secretary of State [Dean Acheson] to the President, November 7, 1952

> [Secretary] indicated if Mosadeq rejects present oil proposal we do not intend to make another believing under this contingency oil question shld [sic] be held in suspect. Under such situation large scale US financing Mosadeq Govt not contemplated. Mosadeq shld not receive a premium for acting as he has. There shld be no large US purchases oil. However, we shld be tolerant of minor measures sufficient to keep Mosadeq barely afloat and thus attempt avoid disastrous possibility of Communists replacing him.[24]
>
> —The Secretary of State [John Foster Dulles] to the Embassy in the United Kingdom, March 7, 1953

In August 1953, Eisenhower went a step beyond merely keeping Mossadeq afloat. With the CIA and the British intelligence services handling logistics, Eisenhower and British Foreign Secretary Anthony Eden hatched a coup against Mossadeq. This was not a direct military intervention. Instead it was a highly coordinated internal political revolt and a massive propaganda campaign designed to paint Mossadeq as a communist stooge in order to soften the fact of his eventual removal by members of the Imperial Guard who were loyal to Reza Shah. Kermit Roosevelt, Theodore Roosevelt's grandson, led the CIA effort in the capital city of Tehran.

---

24. Office of the Historian, *Foreign Relations of the United States, 1952–1954, Volume X* (Washington, DC: Government Printing Office, 1989), 518–19, 702.

FIGURE 4.4 A communist newspaper's office equipment is burned in the streets of Tehran on August 19, 1953, during the pro-Shah riot that swept through Iran's capital. After a day of fighting, Royalist forces triumphed and Prime Minister Mohammad Mossadegh was ousted.

Source: iranianarchives.org. Public Domain.

CIA operatives planted articles in major American and Iranian newspapers claiming that the Tudeh had infiltrated Mossadeq's National Front coalition and was poised to launch an armed communist insurrection on behalf of the Soviet Union. The coup's planners knew these claims to be false. As Figure 4.4 demonstrates, the propaganda campaign created sufficient confusion in which to bring about regime change. To top it off, the Imperial Guard trucked farmworkers into Tehran to fabricate an image of widespread urban revolt against Mossadeq for television and radio consumption.

For his part, Reza Shah gave approval to remove Mossadeq. But when the Imperial guardsmen showed up to arrest the prime minister, Mossadeq instead had the guardsmen arrested. Reza Shah, once poised to reassert royal authority, fled to Baghdad, Iraq. It seemed as if the coup had failed. As word spread throughout Iran, popular resolve swelled behind Mossadeq, particularly from members of the Tudeh who had once been at odds with the nationalist hero.

In light of shifting developments, the CIA changed course. The American ambassador Loy Henderson reached out to Mossadeq with an offer of financial assistance if Mossadeq would call in army brigades to clear the streets of nationalist, antiforeign demonstrators. At this point Mossadeq was desperate, and promptly obliged. Little did he know that his nephew General Mohammed Daftari, whom he had appointed chief of police and military governor of Tehran, was secretly aligned with the coup's organizers. On August 19, Daftari's forces executed the original plan. The battle outside Mossadeq's residence resulted in three hundred deaths, Mossadeq's arrest, and the restoration of the monarchy.

Even with Mossadeq now neutralized, the propaganda campaign forged on with claims that a "popular revolt" against Mossadeq's "antiforeign," "mob rule" had wistfully restored the supposedly "liberal," "progressive" Shah. Eisenhower praised the change in government as the patriotic work of ordinary Iranians and members of the army who had valiantly resisted communist takeover. The coup was, according to its organizers, not a coup at all. It was a triumph of democracy.

Shortly after the events of August 1953, Reza Shah approved an oil concession for a consortium of foreign companies. The National Iranian Oil Company established by Mossadeq continued operations, but it was now under the directive of a 40 percent share for Anglo-Iranian (renamed British Petroleum), 14 percent for Royal Dutch Shell, 6 percent for the French state oil company, and 40 percent to a group of American companies. Nationalization was dead. The new deal featured profit sharing in line with Saudi Arabia's 50–50 agreement with Aramco, $73 million in direct US aid to the Shah, and a reminder about how to repay his political debt to the Americans: crush Iranian communists with massive repression, including imprisonment, torture, and execution.[25]

The long-term consequences of the Mossadeq coup have been profound. Iranians increasingly perceived the United States as simply another colonial power. The US's Cold War imperatives trumped Iranian aspirations for broad-based democratic politics and national self-determination. Reza Shah's increasingly brutal US-backed dictatorship violently repressed its opposition, ultimately laying the political groundwork for the rise of the virulently anti-American Ayatollah Khomeini in 1979. During the hostage crisis of 1979–1981, the "humiliating treatment of American diplomats," as Khalidi explains, "shocked and angered Americans, who knew little of their country's unpopular history of systematic meddling in Iran."

Following Khomeini's 1979 Islamic revolution, he and his advisors pressured the Organization of Petroleum Exporting Countries (OPEC, formed in 1960) to increase prices of oil on which not just Europeans but, with declining domestic production, now many Americans had come to depend. The hostility between the United States and Iran that many take for granted today, as is evident by the Trump administration's recent assassination of top Iranian General Qassem Soleimani in January 2020, could have turned out quite differently had alternative paths been trod during the early years of the Cold War.[26]

Neighboring Iraqis experienced a similarly devastating check on their democratic aspirations as a result of the Cold War struggle over carbon energy. On July 14, 1958, Iraqi Army Brigadier General Abd al-Karim Qasim led a revolt against

---

25. Ervand Abrahamian, "The 1953 Coup in Iran," *Science & Society* 65, no. 2 (Summer 2001): 197–212.

26. Abrahamian, "The 1953 Coup in Iran," 213; Khalidi, *Sowing Crisis*, 154.

the young monarch Amir Faisal II, whose grandfather the British had helped bring to power in 1921 following the breakup of the Ottoman Empire. That year, modern Iraq was constituted without regard to its complex social relationships and political structures that could not be neatly confined within the national borders drawn by British officials after World War I. Faisal remained a nominal figurehead under the authority of Britain's League of Nations Iraq Mandate until 1932. From that point on, Iraq was in theory a fully sovereign country—except for its oil.

As we have already seen, Britain's primary interests in Iraq concerned the oil fields to which the Iraq Petroleum Company maintained exclusive rights. Upon the occasion of the toppling of Faisal's government by Qasim in 1958, IPC's primary prerogative was to maintain control of its developed and undeveloped concessions inside Iraq.

In contrast, Qasim's government, which relied on oil payments for 60 percent of its total revenues, demanded that IPC relinquish undeveloped concessions. Iraq's government could then either manage that oil through a state-run company or offer it to outside bidders. IPC realized no profits from concessions where it had not yet performed test drills. In fact, IPC had to pay so-called dead rents to Iraq to maintain control over the concessions. But to relinquish that territory would have invited competition that the largest oil companies in the world vehemently opposed. Upon IPC's objection to negotiations, in December 1960, Iraq passed Law 80, which cancelled IPC's 1931 concession save for 0.5 percent of the total: the places on the map where IPC was actually producing oil. Qasim's demands ran counter to the cartel capitalism that had made oil executives and shareholders wildly rich in the first six decades of the twentieth century.[27]

Though it was hardly the assertive nationalization of Mossadeq in Iran, Qasim's demands also ran up against American and British Cold War goals to control oil. The relinquishment of concessions might invite Soviet investment in Iraq's oil fields, given the right offer. The nature of Qasim's government—a coalition of career military officers, communists, Ba`athists (more shortly), Nasserites (Arab nationalists aligned with Egyptian Prime Minister Gamal Abd al-Nasser)—meant Iraqi workers stood a fighting chance to achieve real political influence. The Soviets openly supported Qasim's coalition government as it hoped to develop new allies in the region alongside Egypt's Nasser. This was a situation that American and British oil companies and their respective governments were unwilling to tolerate. The deposed monarchy—iron-fisted and decidedly undemocratic—had been IPC's preference, just as the Shah had been AOIC's preference in Iran.

---

27. The details of negotiations over concession relinquishment are meticulously detailed in Samir Saul, "Masterly Inactivity as Brinksmanship: The Iraq Petroleum Company's Route to Nationalization, 1958–1972," *International History Review* 29, no. 4 (December 2007): 746–92; Mitchell, *Carbon Democracy*, 149.

As in Iran, British and American officials began to discuss regime change. As British ambassador to Iraq Roger Allen noted in 1962, "There is now no hope of our ever coming to terms with [Qasim] on major issues, or with Iraq so long as he remains in power." His comments followed two failed assassination attempts against Qasim in 1959 and 1960, both jointly organized by the United States and Britain.[28]

In February 1963, Qasim was in fact murdered in a CIA-backed coup that brought Ba`athists to power. The Ba`ath Party has a complex history that we cannot cover here in detail. Suffice it to say that in Iraq, despite its stated goals of advancing a kind of Pan-Arab socialism, which might lead us to assume sympathy with the Iraq Communist Party, the Ba`ath Party was not sympathetic to communism in any ideological sense. Arab socialism as articulated by the Arab Socialist Ba`ath Party's founder Michel Aflaq (1910–1989), was really an assertion of Arab nationalism, not the advancement of Soviet-style communism. Even so, the USSR preserved relations with the new Ba`athist government, often looking the other way when it ruthlessly murdered leftists, including members of the popular and well-organized Iraq Communist Party.

Ba`athists often worked from CIA-provided kill lists. In 1968, they consolidated power under the presidency of Ahmad Hasan al-Bakr. The Party's strongman, Saddam Hussein, who'd been on the trigger-end of the failed 1959 assassination attempt against Qasim, initiated another round of bloody murders of Iraqi communists. In 1977, protests by Iraq's Shi`i Muslim population against the government's refusal to allow an annual religious commemoration swelled to a more widespread resistance to the Ba`athists' stranglehold on Iraqi civil society. Security forces responded to the protests with overwhelming force. The government executed some of the resistance leaders. In order to reassert its authority, Ba`athist leadership dismissed judges thought to have handed down sentences that were too lenient.

It was in this context of revolt and retribution that Saddam Hussein assumed the presidency in 1979, just after he purged scores of Ba`athist officials suspected of disloyalty.[29] That same year, with the US-backed Reza Shah swept away by the Iranian Revolution, the United States encouraged Hussein to launch an invasion of its neighbor. The Iran-Iraq War, which commenced with Hussein's invasion of Iran in September 1980, escalated US assistance to Iraq, including supplies of chemical weapons that Hussein's forces unleashed not only on Iranian troops but also on Iraq's Kurdish ethnic minority.

---

28. Allen quoted in Saul, "Masterly Inactivity as Brinksmanship," 763; Khalidi, *Sowing Crisis*, 198–99.

29. Mitchell, *Carbon Democracy*, 149; Khalidi, *Sowing Crisis*, 199; Yergin, *The Prize*, 708–09; Charles Tripp, *The Power and the People: Paths of Resistance in the Middle East* (New York: Cambridge University Press, 2013), 76–77.

At the height of the conflict, the United States was providing Hussein with $500 million per year in military aid. In 1990 Hussein used that firepower to invade Kuwait, prompting the United States to retaliate against its now former ally, lest Kuwait's oil come under Iraqi control. Over ten thousand US troops were exposed to US-produced nerve gas when American forces blew up an Iraqi chemical weapons facility during the 1991 Gulf War. In the decade that followed, relentless US bombing coupled with economic sanctions that crippled water treatment, healthcare, and electrical generation facilities resulted in over a million "peacetime" Iraqi deaths, including at least 500,000 children.[30]

In stark contrast to Iran and Iraq, both of which were on the receiving end of Western coups, Saudi Arabia was free of such interventions throughout the Cold War. Indeed, it remains a close ally of the United States today. As a consequence, the Saudi regime has also remained relatively free from any serious consequences for its grave human rights abuses or for its active support of terrorist networks, including al-Qaeda, the group responsible for the attacks of September 11, 2001. What produced this different outcome, given that the stakes for oil production were mutually high in all three countries?

A multitude of factors weigh on the historical US-Saudi relationship during the Cold War. For example, Ibn Saud, eager to weaken regional rivals in neighboring Yemen after the collapse of the Ottoman Empire, signed onto an alliance with Britain in the 1930s that compelled subordination from Yemen's most powerful leader Imam Yahya. The move revealed Ibn Saud's keen ability to use foreign powers for his own ends and to avoid becoming subordinate to them.[31] Saud's pragmatism extended into the Cold War era, where he and his descendants, including his son Faisal bin Abdulaziz (r. 1964–1975), positioned themselves in stark contrast to the more radical Arab nationalist Gamal Abd al-Nasser of Egypt. The House of Saud was ever careful to present an air of independence from Western powers to garner credibility among fellow Arabs. Saudi calls for Palestinian self-determination and the dissolution of the state of Israel remained at the top of this list. But the Saud family also remained staunchly anticommunist, which allowed it to invite Western assistance when necessary. In short, the Saudi royal family deftly maneuvered the politics of the Cold War in ways that strengthened its position.[32]

Finally, the kingdom's deeply conservative, reactionary brand of Islam, known in the West as Wahhabism, has largely stood as an island amidst a much more

---

30. Mahmood Mandani, *Good Muslim, Bad Muslim: America, the Cold War, and the Roots of Terror* (New York: RandomHouse, 2004), 180–83, 190.

31. Isa Blumi, *Destroying Yemen: What Chaos in Arabia Tells Us About the World* (Berkeley: University of California Press, 2019), 48.

32. Naif bin Hethlain, *Saudi Arabia and the US since 1962: Allies in Conflict* (London: Saqi Books, 2010), 37–42. Britain too harnessed Wahhabism in its quest to defeat Imam Yahya in Yemen. See Blumi, *Destroying Yemen*, 43–47.

secular, welcoming Arab world. Saudi-style Islam then, appealed to US policymakers as a uniquely strong bulwark against communism, which the United States often deliberately confused with secular nationalism. Ibn Saud shared such sentiment. In particular, the king believed that the presence of Soviet Jews in Israel (created in 1948) was a communist plot to infiltrate the geographic center of the Islamic world. US officials were, if not in agreement with this sentiment, at least willing to tolerate it in accordance with their own anticommunist tendencies. In 1952, for example, the Saudi government refused to allow a plane carrying American Jews to refuel at Dhahran en route to India. In their official correspondence, US State Department officials seemed more concerned about the potential public relations blowback should the story leak to the American press than about Saudi antisemitism.[33] To this day, America's two closest allies in the region—Saudi Arabia and Israel—remain rhetorically at odds with each other while also bolstering and benefitting from US economic and security interests, including the oil supply.

As we turn to the late- and post–Cold War periods in the next chapter, what do we make of the early Cold War politics of oil in Iran, Iraq, and Saudi Arabia? Americans and Europeans today are often presented with an image of the Middle East replete with autocratic rulers who use extraordinary oil profits to suppress democracy and fund terrorism. The problem, standard scholarly and popular accounts of Middle East oil often assume, is the excess money derived from the production of oil, the so-called oil curse.[34] Kings like Ibn Saud and Reza Shah or secular dictators like Saddam Hussein bought obedience through material development or sufficiently armed security forces capable of violently repressing internal rebellion. Their successors, we are told, continue to do so today.

But this picture obscures, sometimes intentionally, the direct role that the governments and corporations of oil-consuming nations in Europe and North America played in bringing about undemocratic forms of government in the Middle East. They did so by leveraging the pitched Cold War battle between capitalism and communism into a referendum on the outcome of decolonization: communism = tyranny, while capitalism = democracy. The equations were mere propaganda of the *Desert Venture* variety. But they continue to have serious and even deadly consequences for people across the Middle East.

In chapter 5 we turn to the ways in which these false equations allowed oil companies and their government allies to expand the terrain on which they operated, and to maintain political power through the end of the Cold War and beyond. They did so by creating and sustaining an illusion of perpetual global energy shortage and crisis.

---

33. Thomas Lippman, *Inside the Mirage: America's Fragile Partnership with Saudi Arabia* (Boulder, CO: Westview Press, 2004), 213–15.

34. The most widely circulated of this kind is Yergin, *The Prize*.

FURTHER READING

Cooper, Andrew Scott. *The Oil Kings: How the U.S., Iran, and Saudi Arabia Changed the Balance of Power in the Middle East.* New York: Simon & Schuster, 2011.

Heiss, Mary Ann. *Empire and Nationhood: The United States, Great Britain, and Iranian Oil, 1950–1954.* New York: Columbia University Press, 1997.

Khalidi, Rashid. *Sowing Crisis: The Cold War and American Dominance in the Middle East.* Boston: Beacon, 2009.

Latham, Michael. *The Right Kind of Revolution: Modernization: Development, and U.S. Foreign Policy from the Cold War to the Present.* Ithaca, NY: Cornell University Press, 2011.

Painter, David. "Oil and the American Century." *Journal of American History* 99, no. 1 (June 2012): 24–39.

Parker, Chad. *Making the Desert Modern: Americans, Arabs, and Oil on the Saudi Frontier, 1933–1973.* Amherst: University of Massachusetts Press, 2015.

5 THE POLITICS OF ENERGY CRISIS

We thank God
Ken Saro-Wiwa, the star of the morning
The eye of the blind
The leg of the cripple
The bright day light of Ogoni
We welcome you

—Movement for the survival of the ogoni people, "Ken Saro-Wiwa,
the Star of Ogoni," undated

Seattle Times, October 9, 1973: "Six of the biggest oil-producing countries in the world opened the second stage today of a campaign to force an immediate 66 per cent increase in prices paid by Western oil companies. Oil sources said the demand could result in the biggest leap in crude-oil prices in two years, a move almost certain to affect the American consumer. The sources said the price-hike demand was presented yesterday to 13 Western companies by six states on the Persian Gulf, members of the Organization of Petroleum Exporting Countries."[1]

Robert Hager, *NBC News*, October 11, 1973: "Even before the meeting began, there was announcement in Kuwait that the prices for Arab oil were going up: a huge increase voted in an overnight meeting without even consulting Western buyers. Then the [oil] ministers began what was to be an eight-hour meeting, resulting in their decision to reduce the flow of oil to America and other nations supporting Israel. The cutback will be five percent for the first month and an additional five percent each passing month until

---

1. "Price Boost Asked," *Seattle Times*, October 9, 1973.

Israeli forces leave occupied Arab land. The ministers added an appeal to the American people to stand beside the Arab world."[2]

Robert Lindsey, *New York Times*, December 25, 1973: "The Arab oil embargo hit Lewisboro in northern Westchester County [New York] last week. Dozens of schoolchildren who were accustomed to being picked up each morning near their homes were told that they must walk up to a mile farther to catch the bus. The reason is that the fuel deliveries to the Katonah-Lewisboro School District were cut by 14 per cent."[3]

In late 1973 and early 1974, many Americans feared the United States would soon run out of oil. As Figure 5.1 shows, many filling stations did. Even schoolchildren endured undue hardship. The culprits seemed obvious to anyone who watched the nightly network news or read the morning paper: Arab oil-producing states.

In October 1973, these states collectively launched a two-pronged assault on American oil consumption: an increase in price and a decrease in production. According to the economic doctrine of supply and demand, decreased production was sure to further increase prices. The panic spurred rushes to filling stations, where owners raised prices, imposed rations, ran out of gasoline, or some combination of the three.

FIGURE 5.1 Bird's-eye view of a gas station in Portland, Oregon, 1973.

---

2. NBC Nightly News, John Chancellor, anchor, October 11, 1973, YouTube, https://www.youtube.com/watch?v=VCLRIVxOH-Q.

3. Robert Lindsey, "School Bus Service Hit by Fuel Crisis and Prices," *New York Times*, December 25, 1973.

The experience established a bitterness toward Arab countries unimaginable in the heyday of Aramco's partnership with Saudi Arabia. By the time Arab member-states of the Organization of Petroleum Exporting Countries (OPEC, established 1960) lifted the embargo in March 1974, the United States' relationship to the Middle East had changed dramatically. For many Americans, Arabs had become enemies. Just over a quarter-century after its release, *Desert Venture* now seemed an arcane and naive image of US-Arab relations.

The problem with this account of the so-called energy crisis of 1973–1974 was that it never actually happened.[4] Or, at least it did not happen in the way that news outlets, government officials, and oil experts frequently presented it to ordinary consumers.

Typical characterizations often went like this: Arab producer states used oil as a political weapon to force the United States to pressure Israel to withdraw its military from territories it had occupied in Palestine, Egypt, and Syria since June 1967. In October 1973, OPEC announced an increase in the price of oil that Western oil companies had to pay to acquire it. Simultaneously, Saudi Arabia announced 5 percent cutbacks per month in oil supply to the United States until an Israeli withdrawal was in the offing. Critics referred to these tactics as the "oil weapon." The implication was that Arab governments alone had disruptively intervened in the global oil market for self-serving, unrelated political reasons.

All of this did indeed happen, except the Israeli withdrawal from Palestine. But it is not what created the so-called energy crisis—the American national panic about unaffordable and increasingly insecure energy. The crisis had more to do with the ways in which the largest American oil firms—no longer producers in most cases but instead buyers, transporters, and short-term contractors in the Middle East oil industry—along with the US government and American media outlets, chose to characterize OPEC's demands. These choices were rarely if ever covered in as much detail as the initial decision by Arab oil ministers to issue price hikes and supply reductions.

A focus on one set of political actors (producer states) and not others (international oil companies and Western governments) significantly transformed America's and Western Europe's relationship to the Middle East. So what did happen with carbon energy in 1973 that would have lasting impacts for politics, economics, and environment through the end the Cold War and into the twenty-first century?

As its title suggests, this book's final chapter examines the politics surrounding the so-called energy crisis of 1973–1974. It involved not any real physical shortage of energy (oil or otherwise) but instead a political crisis that brought to an end the near complete post–World War II dominance of Western oil companies. But for the rest of the twentieth century, near complete dominance gave way, in most cases, to outsized influence nonetheless.

Forced earlier to abandoned their total control over Middle East oil, the embargo of 1973–1974 prompted the oil giants to devise novel ways to re-direct the

---

4. Timothy Mitchell, *Carbon Democracy: Political Power in the Age of Oil* (London: Verso, 2013), 173–75.

flow of oil payments back to the United States and Europe and to pursue new, environmentally riskier locations for energy production. In doing so, they secured arrangements in, for example, sub-Saharan Africa, Latin America, and Southeast Asia. After the breakup of the Soviet Union in 1991, the largest oil companies were there, knocking on the doors of government offices in Azerbaijan, Kazakhstan, and Georgia to secure energy contracts previously unavailable during the Cold War.

The companies also expanded the scope of their energy portfolios beyond oil to include gas, coal, and uranium. They even began to express public concern over the environmental impacts of energy production. The manufactured energy crisis of 1973–1974 had lasting impacts on the politics of carbon energy for the rest of the twentieth century and into the twenty-first.

Before we address the long-term transformations produced by the Arab oil embargo of 1973–1974, we must first consider the historical developments that gave rise to it. With over two decades of voracious oil consumption preceding it, the crisis of 1973–1974 indeed seemed to come out of nowhere. Between 1948 and 1972, Western Europe's oil consumption rose from 970,000 to 14,100,000 barrels a day, a fifteen-fold increase. In postwar Japan, consumption climbed from a meager 32,000 to 4,400,000 million barrels a day during the same period. Like Western Europe, all of it was imported.

Though not the site of the most dramatic rise (it was already a massive consumer and producer), the United States too increased its oil dependency. Consumption tripled between 1948 and 1972, in no small part because the US government constructed an interstate highway system, did not regulate vehicle fuel economy standards, and imposed import controls on foreign oil that kept smaller domestic producers relatively competitive.

Though international oil companies appreciated any government policy that encouraged consumption, regulatory measures often incensed firms like Texaco, Chevron, and Exxon, who produced oil in the Middle East and elsewhere. Their executives preferred to set prices and to determine supply levels using cartel arrangements. At least that was the public stance they often took.

In reality, the international firms benefited from government restrictions on cheaper imports. They could sell domestically produced oil at higher prices and control foreign production costs. Despite their rhetoric about the sanctity of free enterprise, these companies preferred government-aided global monopoly over competition.

Their reservations aside, relatively affordable prices coupled with steady supply meant that the industrial world first built with coal now relied primarily on flows of oil.[5] Throughout the 1950s and 1960s, that oil supply seemed

---

5. Daniel Yergin, *The Prize: The Epic Quest for Oil, Money, and Power* (New York: Simon & Schuster, 1991), 541–42; Paul Sabin, "Crisis and Continuity in U.S. Oil Politics, 1965–1980," *Journal of American History*, 99, no. 1 (June 2012): 177–79.

endless to the average consumer. Yet in the early 1970s confidence in the abundance and affordability of oil eroded, culminating in the energy crisis of 1973–1974. What happened?

Posted Prices

On the surface, the lead-up to the oil embargo of 1973–1974 reads like a classic Cold War tale of economic warfare. Desperate to increase revenues, in 1955 the Soviet Union began advertising ultra-cheap oil to potential Western European buyers. Between 1955 and 1960, Soviet production doubled. Since there was no domestic production to protect, British Petroleum (BP), Royal Dutch Shell (usually known as Shell), Total (France), and others could not easily pressure their governments to impose import quotas to keep Soviet oil out. Consumers clamored for cheap oil.

The Soviet Union hoped to flood the Western European market and undercut prices dictated by the international (mostly US-based) companies. Since the late 1940s, Western Europe's oil came primarily from Iran, Iraq, and Saudi Arabia, with smaller quantities supplied by Egypt, Libya, Algeria, and Kuwait. The American producers in the Middle East, along with BP, actively encouraged Europe's energy conversion from coal to oil as a way to tap this emerging market. In turn European governments benefitted from the conversion's threat to organized labor, which had been particularly effective in the coal industry. New oil supplies from the Communist Bloc threatened to undermine the primacy of American and European producers operating in the Middle East. It could, if left unchecked, also lead to a resurgence in European radical labor movements whose participants were skeptical of governments' collusion with corporations.

Facing increased Soviet market competition—an ironic description given American depictions of the USSR as anticapitalist—the international oil companies faced two main options. One option was to respond by lowering the "market" price of Middle East oil. In doing so, the companies would meet the Soviet challenge but absorb the profit shortfalls alone. One need not hold an economics degree to imagine how company executives felt about this.

Or, they could lower the "posted" price of oil that the largest American companies had set since the 1930s. The posted price had always hinged on US government regulation that kept domestic producers from having to operate at costs higher than the market return on a barrel of oil. Stability, not cutthroat competition, was the point. Production and import limits had protected US domestic producers from ruin since 1934. That protection also meant instability for foreign producer states like Iran or the South American oil giant Venezuela. These governments relied heavily on taxation of oil exports to the United States and Europe.

If the international firms responded to Soviet competition by lowering the posted price, producer states would shoulder a greater loss share, thus protecting corporate profits. To that point, tax revenues or "rents" paid by oil companies to producer governments were determined according to the posted price. A lower posted price meant decreased tax revenue, while a lower market price meant decreased corporate profits.

This seemingly simple choice between two economic decisions faced by the international companies has dominated much of the analysis of postwar oil politics. In particular, it has helped to explain the backlash from Arab producer states. Shortly after the 1973–1974 crisis, Peter Odell asserted that "the producing countries were made painfully aware of this danger [of increased supplies of Soviet oil] in the late 1950s when the potential oil surplus and the need to stimulate demand persuaded the companies to announce significant overall reductions in the prices they 'posted' for crude oils."[6] Similarly, in his sprawling account of the twentieth-century politics of oil, Daniel Yergin asked: "Could they dare cut the posted price as well, so that the producing countries would share the burdens of competing with the Russians?"[7] And despite the rich diplomatic historical analysis offered by Nathan Citino, he presents the 1959 decision by Arab governments to send representatives to Cairo, Egypt for an oil congress as a "response to the decline in oil prices."[8]

These scholars are not wrong about outrage at the companies' use of posted price reductions. But each of these explanations assume that the posted price was a real function of economics—something actually related to the cost of producing, refining, transporting, and marketing oil. It was not.

Recent scholarship has offered clarification on this point. Francisco Parra has described the decision by the international oil companies to reduce the posted price in 1959 as the removal of an artificial "barrier" that for at least ten years had "insulated [producer governments, like Saudi Arabia and Iraq] from market pressure." In short, Parra asserts that price formulations used up through the 1960s—the so-called posted price of a barrel of crude oil—"were, as prices, an economic fiction."[9] Likewise, Timothy Mitchell concludes that the news media and American public were "unaware that the 'posted price' was simply a device for calculating tax rates." They "assumed these were negotiations over the price of oil. The companies could then portray the increased taxation of their windfall profits from oil as an increase in its 'price'—an increase that they would be obliged to pass on to the consumer."[10]

---

6. Peter Odell, *Oil and World Power: Background to the Oil Crisis* (New York: Taplinger Publishing Company, 1975), 18.

7. Yergin, *The Prize*, 515.

8. Nathan Citino, *From Arab Nationalism to OPEC: Eisenhower, King Sa'ud, and the Making of US-Saudi Relations* (Bloomington: Indiana University Press, 2010), 255.

9. Francisco Parra, *Oil Politics: A Modern History of Petroleum* (London: I. B. Tauris, 2004), 56, 63–64.

10. Mitchell, *Carbon Democracy*, 168, 174.

Put another way, the posted price was merely a way for international oil companies to enjoy profits from oil produced outside the United States at highly regulated domestic prices. It allowed the companies to reap the benefits of economic globalization without actually having to compete in a global marketplace.

The artificial nature of the posted price may have been lost on the average consumer. But oil ministers in the largest producer states outside of the US and USSR were well aware of its function. In 1960, Venezuela, Saudi Arabia, Iran, Iraq, and Kuwait formed OPEC. It was an attempt to assert their collective power in order to gain a more equitable share of oil profits.

OPEC's member states hoped to preserve higher posted prices (and thus higher corporate taxes) even when overproduction drove down the actual market price of oil. Put simply, OPEC "hoped to put production and pricing more in the hands of those who owned the resources."[11] Gone were the days when Aramco and other oil company officials could credibly claim that they were development partners rather than cold imperialists in the Middle East.

OPEC's first decade did not bear much fruit. Saudi oil ministers, for example, failed to force Aramco to increase production as compensation for having lowered the posted price. They did announce suspensions of oil shipments to America and Britain in 1967 in response to their support for Israel's war against Egypt, Jordan, Syria and Lebanon. But it was not until the Libyan oil embargo in 1970 that OPEC really gained the upper hand.[12]

That year, pipeline and tanker port stoppages—some of which resulted from worker sabotage efforts—temporarily prevented Saudi, Iraqi, Kuwaiti, and Iranian oil from reaching its primary market in Western Europe. This helped the brash young Colonel Muammar al-Qaddafi assert nationalist control over Libya's oil. By virtue of geography, Libyan oil could still reach Europe via tanker. With twenty-one American and European companies operating in Libya (which had joined OPEC in 1962), Qaddafi's Deputy Prime Minister Abdel Salaam Ahmed Jalloud singled out the California-based Occidental Petroleum Company.

Occidental was vulnerable. In 1965, it had staked all of its international oil exploration in Libya. A sustained oil embargo against Occidental would have ruined the company's executives. Jalloud's hardline negotiations with CEO Armand Hammer resulted in a 20 percent increase in royalties and taxes paid by Occidental to Qaddafi's government. Negotiations ensued with the other twenty companies. Within a short time, all agreed to boost the artificial posted price of Libyan oil by 30 cents a barrel and to increase Libya's profit sharing from 50 percent to 55 percent. One can imagine just how profitable oil had been for company executives to have agreed to these demands.

---

11. Chad Parker, *Making the Desert Modern: Americans, Arabs, and Oil on the Saudi Frontier, 1933–1973* (Amherst: University of Massachusetts Press, 2015), 121.

12. Mitchell, *Carbon Democracy*, 168.

Qaddafi's successful extraction of major concessions on posted price and profit-sharing signaled a potential sea change in the balance of power between international oil companies and producer states. Following Libya's lead, other OPEC members began demanding and receiving increasingly more favorable arrangements through 1972. When the major international oil companies and the smaller independent companies attempted to present a united front (something they had never before done), producer states responded with either outright nationalization (Iraq, Libya) or negotiations for participation and transfer agreements (Iran, Saudi Arabia). These agreements meant that while the companies still produced oil, they no longer had the final say when it came to pricing and production levels.

The victories of producer states aligned in the early 1970s with a tightening supply–demand balance between the Middle East producer states and their Western consumers. Global petroleum demand was likely to continue its upward trajectory, experts warned. Meanwhile, the import quotas that the Eisenhower administration imposed in 1959 caused the United States to use up its own reserves more quickly than it otherwise might have. Decreasing US reserves and increasing demand in the United States and elsewhere earned OPEC's members newfound positions of political power relative to the international oil companies.[13]

But the companies did not go quietly. Instead, they worked to reorganize the global economy and global energy politics by taking advantage of increasing concerns about limited oil supplies and environmental destruction. The so-called energy crisis of 1973–1974 was critical to selling this reorganization to ordinary oil consumers and government officials. It was in one sense a fabrication designed to distill the actual causes of the oil price hikes into a single explanation that could be pinned on producer states alone. Let us now unpack this reorganization strategy in order to understand how the companies shaped the politics of carbon energy in last quarter of the twentieth century.[14]

Inventing an Energy Crisis

We have just explored the ways that producer states' demands coupled with US import quotas and explosive economic growth allowed international oil firms to use the posted price of oil to raise the actual market price on consumers. Likewise, we saw how American media coverage of the steep spike in oil prices in late 1973 distilled the causes into a simple supply-and-demand explanation. In this version of the story, producer states wielded oil as a political weapon to serve their own

---

13. Yergin, *The Prize*, 577–82, 585–87; Mitchell, *Carbon Democracy*, 167.

14. Mitchell, *Carbon Democracy*, 174.

interests. There was plenty of oil, some in the media claimed, but Arab governments denied it to Western consumers through supply reductions and price increases. Meanwhile, the international companies had already begun to speak about "peak oil"—a future scenario in which the world's oil supplies would dwindle, causing prices to soar. According to the companies, OPEC seemed bent on making the crisis more immediate and acute.

In chapters 3 and 4, we addressed what we can now see with the benefit of historical analysis the irony of these claims. For most of the twentieth century, oil firms worried not about shortages but instead about overproduction, which threatened exorbitant profits. Control, not a frenzy of drilling, was the preferred mode of business. The oil fields of the Middle East—strategic in Cold War terms and also dangerous to high profits should they fall into hands eager to pump as much petroleum as time and labor would allow—were of particular concern at Standard Oil, BP, and Texaco. But by the early 1970s, oil executives openly decried Arab governments that threatened to limit oil supplies.

This historical amnesia—in most cases an unwitting ignorance—by American petroleum consumers provided one of the conditions for the international oil companies to devise new political strategies that allowed them to continue to profit from the dramatic price increases of 1973–1974, even if prices eventually came crashing down, which they did in 1986. Oil executives pretended to commiserate with their customers over the unwelcome Arab oil weapon unleashed on the supposedly free market. But in practice, the companies benefitted immensely from the price hikes, since most people misunderstood them as a function of supply and demand.

However, the façade of Arab collusion could not prop up high profits forever. To do that, the oil companies had to either create or shape other political factors that helped to prop up the industry and to expand its reach into other places and other kinds of fuels, both carbon-based and not. Indeed, the oil companies had already begun laying the groundwork for such a transformation even before OPEC announced its embargo in late 1973.

The first factor seems at first glance one that oil companies would oppose almost instinctively: the rise of the modern environmental movement. At root, modern environmentalists have recognized continuous economic expansion after World War II, whether under capitalism or communism or some other economic arrangement, as inherently threatening to the Earth's ecosystems. If left unchecked, human activity—population growth, mass agriculture, nuclear testing, carpet-bombing, coal mining, oil drilling, consumerism—threatened to alter ecological systems on local and global scales.

No single event caused environmentalism. It did not emerge in a single place and then fan out around the globe. Instead it emerged simultaneously in multiple nations and colonies, with activists very often rallying around specific local environmental problems. Both affluent and poor people participated, sometimes in solidarity, at other times at cross-purposes. Given this complexity, it remains a rich field for historians. We cannot do it justice here.[15]

But suffice it to say that by the late 1960s, environmentalists clearly identified the international oil industry as a central actor in ecological destruction. Dramatic disasters such as the 1967 Torrey Canyon supertanker wreck in the English Channel and the 1969 underwater wellhead blowout off the coast of Santa Barbara, California galvanized environmentalists' calls for increased oversight. Accountability demands extended beyond the consumer societies of North America, Europe, and East Asia to producer states, including Ecuador, Indonesia, and Nigeria. These movements very often intersected with broader demands for what many might today call social justice.[16]

Of course, the oil companies loathed calls for regulation that targeted specific activities like drilling, pipeline transport, or refining. But the rise of modern environmentalism, if channeled away from oil production toward other kinds of environmental threats, could actually serve their interests. It could distract anyone concerned with the broader ecological costs of market- or state-driven industrial extraction from the specific negligence of oil companies.

To do so, oil executives first prompted their economists to completely reverse the conventional wisdom that had prevailed since the 1940s: the idea that there was an endless supply of oil. Abruptly in the early 1970s, oil economists began arguing that oil was in fact going to run out. Only an impressive conservation effort, they now argued, would prevent massive energy shortages and painfully expensive costs.

The forecasts of what came to be called peak oil were false or at best premature. And they failed to account for massive investments in new and increasingly risky oil exploration in ecologically sensitive places like the Arctic Ocean or the Ecuadoran Amazon and to increase offshore drilling (see Figure 5.2). But the language of oil conservation meshed well with the language of environmentalism that spoke of the natural world as something finite that needed to be protected instead of rapaciously exploited. This seemingly subtle shift softened the image of big international oil companies, whose executives now claimed to have taken the interests of the natural world to heart.

But simply rebranding big oil as conservation-minded was not enough. Even an armchair environmentalist could see right through the propaganda. The companies

---

15. For overviews, see for example Ramachandra Guha, *Environmentalism: A Global History* (New York: Longman, 2000); Samuel Hayes, *A History of Environmental Politics Since 1945* (Pittsburgh: University of Pittsburgh Press, 2000).

16. See for example, Robert Bullard, *Dumping in Dixie: Race, Class, and Environmental Quality* (Boulder, CO: Westview Press, 2000); Ike Okonta and Oronto Douglas, *Where Vultures Feast: Shell, Human Rights, and Oil in the Niger Delta* (San Francisco: Sierra Club Books, 2001), Jeffrey Broadbent, *Environmental Politics in Japan: Networks of Power and Protest* (Cambridge: Cambridge University Press, 1998).

FIGURE 5.2 Offshore drilling is the new frontier, c. 1970.
Source: U.S. Department of Energy

needed an environmental threat seemingly greater than their own to deflect political and social pressure. They found that threat in the emerging nuclear power industry.

Billed by its supporters as a cleaner, and in the midst of the spike in oil prices, potentially cheaper alternative to fossil fuels, nuclear power appeared to stand a real chance of replacing coal and oil, particularly for electric power generation. By the 1970s, countries like France, Belgium, Germany, and Japan, which had all relied on imported oil since the 1940s, began shifting to nuclear.[17]

But nuclear power was rife with both economic and environmental risks. To an even greater extent than oil production, nuclear projects gobbled up massive government subsidies and investments. Few private insurers would touch it, and most private investors were skeptical of its eventual profitability. Technical disasters beginning in 1957 in the United Kingdom and culminating in the 1986 Chernobyl disaster in the Soviet Union raised serious concerns about both the short-term and long-term safety of nuclear power.[18] Oil lobbyists seized on these high-profile

17. J. R. McNeill and Peter Engelke, *The Great Acceleration: An Environmental History of the Anthropocene since 1945* (Cambridge, MA: Belknap Press, 2014), 27–28.

18. J. R. McNeill, *Something New Under the Sun: An Environmental History of the Twentieth-Century World* (New York: Norton, 2000), 312–13.

disasters—and downplayed their own—to point out the environmental threats of nuclear energy. It should not, for the Earth's sake, they cautioned, replace oil. Stick with the devil you know, they argued.

Given international oil's critique of nuclear power, the second factor that enabled the oil companies to ride out the alleged energy crisis may seem ironic or disingenuous. Beginning in the 1960s, oil companies began transforming themselves into "total energy" companies. They acquired assets in coal, uranium, and natural gas. In short, they pursued an agenda that put them in control of all major forms of energy, first within the United States and thereafter beyond it.

The coal industry was the first to go. By 1975, 11 of the 15 largest US coal companies had been purchased by either American oil companies or other mining or industrial outfits like Kennicott Copper (Utah) or General Dynamics (Virginia). If they were not busy acquiring coal companies, the oil majors targeted coal reserves as well. From 1962 to 1969, the 15 largest American oil giants gobbled up an additional 12.4 percent of total US coal reserves, increasing their share to 53.3 percent. Similar acquisitions and reserve purchases unfolded in uranium mining. By 1975, oil companies controlled 40 percent of the nation's uranium reserves.[19] If the oil giants spoke publicly about the environmental dangers of nuclear power, their swift control of uranium deposits and other points of nuclear power generation suggested that those warnings were disingenuous.

The Richard Nixon administration further encouraged consolidation by creating the National Energy Office. The NEO, the precursor to today's Department of Energy, commissioned studies designed to make palatable the sustained spike in oil prices. It frequently corroborated oil industry studies that often overestimated future US needs by as much as 60 percent in order to thwart competition from other energy sectors. Sometimes these efforts failed, as they did in 1968 when oil companies unsuccessfully sought a natural gas rate increase from the Federal Power Commission. The oil companies, which had acquired controlling shares in rival power sources, simply announced supply reductions for natural gas in order to create the intended rise in the price of oil. The Arab oil weapon, as pundits often called it, was apparently a favorite tool of the oil companies themselves.[20]

But we might also interpret the oil giants' embrace of environmentalist language and its simultaneous foray into coal, gas, and uranium production as a shrewd hedge against the very real political volatility present in many of the largest oil-producing countries in the Middle East. Collectively, they had come to dominate oil production in the twenty-five years since the end of World War II. By 1970, the companies had all been forced to accede to Qaddafi's demands in Libya for a much larger piece of the pie. If such volatility troubled the executives at American

19. Joe Stork, *Middle East Oil and the Energy Crisis* (New York: Monthly Review Press, 1975), 121–22.

20. Mitchell, *Carbon Democracy*, 179–80.

oil companies like Socal, Gulf, and Exxon, they devised new ways of softening these threats to their profits. They reversed previous projections about oil supply in order to create a false picture of limited energy resources. They then channeled the profits back into consolidation of other forms of energy and into expensive exploration and development projects that further threatened ecosystems that the companies now claimed to steward.

By the mid-1970s, the Cold War struggle for political dominance over Middle East oil had been both won and lost from the perspective of the biggest US oil firms. Yes, they had ceded some decision-making power to state-owned companies in the largest oil-producing states in the region, including Saudi Arabia, Iraq, Iran, and Libya. But much of the state revenues that resulted from these changes flowed back to the United States in the form of US Treasury bond purchases and the opening of enormous new bank accounts with the biggest financial institutions in New York and London. Windfall profits required that the oligarchs in the oil-producing states stash revenues away in more secure currencies and banks, lest popular forces within their own societies demand a greater redistribution of the oil rents.[21]

Profits also returned via large military contracts by the United States' biggest weapons producers—contracts that helped to maintain both an illusion of security over the oil fields and a state of perpetual political insecurity in the region that would require continued arms transfers far into the future. Oil companies received handsome rewards in the form of major tax breaks and unprecedented political influence in the White House and on Capitol Hill. That savings and influence could, if necessary, be leveraged in the pursuit of new carbon energy projects in the United States and around the world in the last quarter of the twentieth century and into the twenty-first.

The so-called energy crisis was in hindsight pivotal in creating and sustaining a series of conflicts in the Middle East that stretches from the early 1970s to today. While not the sole cause, the energy crisis spurred on the expansion of the US Defense Department's budget and promoted the growth of large weapons manufacturers. But these conflicts also made quite obvious to the executives of the major US oil companies—and of course international oil companies based outside of the United States—the inherent "risks associated with having too many eggs in a single Middle Eastern basket."[22] Nationalizations by OPEC member states meant increasing reliance on just a handful of controllable fields. That realization in large part shaped global energy politics through century's end.[23]

---

21. F. William Engdahl, *A Century of War: Anglo-American Oil Politics and the New World Order* (London: Pluto, 2004), 155.

22. Duncan Clarke, *Crude Continent: The Struggle for Africa's Oil Prize* (London: Profile Books, 2008), 75.

23. James Marriott and Mika Minio-Paluello, *The Oil Road: Journeys from the Caspian Sea to the City of London* (New York: Verso, 2013), 18.

In the century's final decades, the pretext of energy crisis allowed the international energy companies to expand the geographic scope of their operations. Their continued reliance on undemocratic methods and unelected governments as the most viable way to ensure steady access to energy, meant that hard-won freedom from foreign rule in places like the Federal Republic of Nigeria (from Britain, 1960) or the Republic of Azerbaijan (from USSR, 1991) was reduced to authoritarian or military rule. Oil remained a hindrance to democratic politics and a lubricant for authoritarianism.

Neocolonial Carbon

By all basic economic measures, the west African country of Nigeria emerged in the last quarter of the twentieth century as a "petrostate," dependent primarily on oil exports for basic operations. In 1992, oil from the Niger River Delta made up a fourth of Nigeria's gross domestic product. Fifteen years later, it was half, with 80 percent of government revenues derived from oil. By contrast, in 1967, oil revenues accounted for 30 percent of the national budget.[24]

Historians who study Africa debate the degree to which oil development caused the Nigerian civil war that began in 1967, when the oil-rich state of Biafra attempted secession. But they do agree that oil had a decisive impact on the course and outcomes of the civil war far beyond the end of major military hostilities in 1970. During the civil war, military generals and government bureaucrats asserted greater national control over oil production and marketing. Oil was to be the main ingredient for a nation-building project that united Nigerians under an all-powerful central government (see Map 5.1).

Those military generals in power in the capital city of Lagos implemented partial nationalization of Nigeria's oil industry (1969). In 1971, they established the Nigerian National Oil Company (NNOC) to handle the marketing and distribution of oil. World oil prices soon soared as result of the energy crisis of 1973–1974. Nigeria's oil production—dominated by a joint venture between Shell and BP since the 1950s—ballooned to over two million barrels a day. In short order, the central government, once poor and enthralled to British colonial interests, was now flush with oil money. Independence seemed within reach.[25]

As the country began to absorb windfall revenues from oil over the course of the 1970s, control over the oil fields and pipelines became critical to anyone with

---

24. Okonta and Douglas, *Where Vultures Feast*, 18; Okey Ibeanu and Robin Luckham, "Nigeria: Political Violence, Governance, and Corporate Responsibility in a Petro-state," in *Oil Wars*, ed. Mary Kaldor, Terry Lynn Karl, and Yahia Said (Ann Arbor, MI: Pluto Press, 2007), 41.

25. Ibeanu and Luckham, "Nigeria," 45, 47.

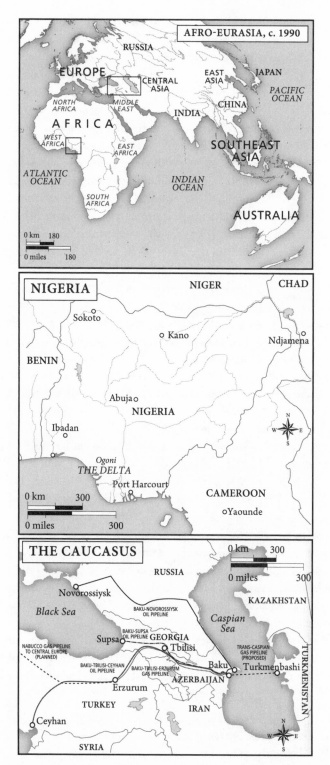

MAP 5.1 Afro-Eurasia, c. 1990, with insets of Nigeria and the Caucasus

political aspirations. In 1975, the military regime issued Decree 6, which increased the central government's share of oil revenues from 50 percent to 80 percent. It left the country's twelve states with 20 percent to divide among themselves. A series of military generals began distributing oil revenues to themselves and their oligarchic partners at the expense of locals in the Niger Delta, Nigeria's chief oil-producing region.

With so many petrodollars accumulating in government coffers, temptations for corruption abounded. The personal bank accounts of various military generals— the coups and countercoups against which we have not the time to detail here— swelled to obscene levels. Repeated economic Development Plans in 1970–1974 and 1975–1980 called for massive investments of the oil revenues into education, infrastructure, healthcare, and other public projects. Few of those noble outcomes materialized. A class of political parasites who were involved in neither the production, transport, or marketing of the country's oil, profited immensely from its sale on the global market.

Corruption made worse the near wholesale neglect of Nigeria's agricultural sector. Largely self-sufficient in farming capacity in 1960, Nigeria became increasingly dependent on food imports as the oil flowed outward in greater volumes after 1970. From 1972 to 1974, peasants faced starvation when drought threatened their already meager food production. Add to this environmental crisis, the luxury to which top government officials became accustom combined with a sharp rise in Federal Public Service employee salaries to create monetary inflation. Declining food production and inflation meant that the poorest could not afford the food imports upon which Nigeria now depended.[26]

The 1980s provided little respite. Added to the problem of systemic corruption was the government's ballooning foreign debt. When General Muhammadu Buhari assumed power in late 1983, his government carried over $16 billion in debt from his predecessor Shehu Shegari, the centerpiece of which was a $480 million deal with British Aerospace for a fleet of eighteen Jaguar ground-attack fighters. Heavy investments in military hardware were not simply for national defense. The central government increasingly used violence against Nigerian citizens who challenged its authority. We've seen how similar deals between US weapons manufacturers and Middle Eastern autocrats—facilitated by US oil companies—promoted similar states of perpetual emergency in the region's oil-producing countries. Nigeria followed a similar course.

Internal corruption, while rampant and exceedingly damaging to Nigeria's economic, political, and literal health, was not simply the outcome of Nigeria's increasing dependence on oil exports. External pressures abounded too. In 1986,

26. Okonta and Douglas, *Where Vultures Feast*, 25; Douglas A Yates, *The Scramble for African Oil: Oppression, Corruption, and War for Control of Africa's Natural Resources* (London: Pluto Press, 2012), 210.

Newswatch, Nigeria's premiere English-language newspaper, revealed that not only was 20 percent of Nigeria's oil being smuggled out of the country illegally by militia groups and members of the national army and navy. Western creditors often demanded repayment of debts that were the result of a fraud scheme hatched by British bankers, Asian merchants, and Nigerian government officials. Bankers in London pressed the US-controlled International Monetary Fund (IMF) to force Nigeria to accept a $5 billion short-term loan to pay back the debt—more debt to pay back fraudulent debt![27]

In exchange for the loan, the International Monetary Fund (IMF) demanded that Nigeria abide by a Structural Adjustment Program (SAP), central features of which are currency devaluation, elimination of tariffs on foreign imports, and privatization of publicly held state assets like water treatment plants, electrical grids, and schools. As numerous examples from the mid-1970s onward have shown, IMF-imposed SAPs have deepened and widened, not eased poverty in the formerly colonized world.[28]

Nigeria was no exception. Amidst growing popular pressure, Buhari attempted to ease the country's mounting foreign debt by exchanging oil for key imports from countries outside the influence of the IMF. Despite his autocratic regime, Buhari seemed to recognize that Nigeria could not go on as it had been, with foreign debt and rampant corruption as the central features of its oil economy. In response, the foreign banks, the international oil companies, and their local counterparts in the national oil company responded with a coup in 1985.

Buhari's replacement, General Ibrahim Babangida, repaid the favor by accepting the SAP in 1986, which further entrenched poverty in the urban slums in Lagos and in the rural countryside.[29] When global oil prices skyrocketed in 1990 as a result of the American military offensive against Iraq, Babangida used most of the windfall profits not for foreign debt repayment or development projects. Instead, the money went to embassy expense accounts, international travel, and a $3 million documentary film that attributed Nigeria's historical path out of colonialism to the benevolent rule of the general himself.[30]

The elevated levels of poverty that only deepened under Babangida's IMF-imposed economic "adjustments" gave rise to more pronounced if not entirely new popular resistance. Led by former Rivers state education commissioner Ken Saro-Wiwa, a mass movement against the collusion between Shell-BP, the IMF, and the Nigerian government began in earnest in August 1990. The Movement for the Survival of the Ogoni People (MOSOP), which combined environmental

---

27. Okonta and Douglas, *Where Vultures Feast*, 30.

28. Mike Davis, *Planet of Slums* (London: Verso, 2007), 151–73.

29. Okonta and Douglas, *Where Vultures Feast*, 31.

30. Wale Akin Aina, "Pandora's Box," *Newswatch*, January 16, 1995, 9–14.

justice with human rights politics, issued an Ogoni Bill of Rights. The document was remarkable for its clarity of purpose and its attention to the historical injustices wrought by corporate oil and the military government in the Niger Delta:

> We, the people of Ogoni . . . numbering about 500,000 being a separate and distinct ethnic nationality within the Federal Republic of Nigeria wish to draw the attention of the Governments and people of Nigeria to the undermentioned facts:
>
> . . . That in over 30 years of oil mining, the Ogoni nationality have provided the Nigerian nation with a total revenue estimated at over 40 billion Naira . . . or 30 billion dollars.
>
> That in return for the above contribution, the Ogoni people have received NOTHING.
>
> That today, the Ogoni people have:
>
> No representation whatsoever in ALL institutions of the Federal Government of Nigeria;
>
> No pipe-borne water;
>
> No electricity;
>
> No job opportunities for the citizens in Federal, State, public sector or private sector companies;
>
> No social or economic project of the Federal Government . . .
>
> That the search for oil has caused severe land and food shortages in Ogoni, one of the most densely populated areas of Africa . . .
>
> That neglectful environmental pollution laws and substandard inspection techniques of the Federal authorities have led to the complete degradation of the Ogoni environment, turning our homeland into an ecological disaster . . .
>
> That it is intolerable that one of the richest areas of Nigeria should wallow in abject poverty and destitution . . .
>
> That the Ogoni people wish to manage their own affairs.[31]

Though it primarily focused on Ogoni self-determination in Nigeria, MOSOP's leaders made clear how the Ogoni struggle was international in scope. In a forward penned in late 1991 after the Bill of Rights' initial release, Saro-Wiwa wrote of MOSOP's urgent intentions:

> It is the intention of the Ogoni people to draw the attention of the American government and people to the fact that the oil which they buy from Nigeria is stolen property and that it is against American law to receive stolen goods . . .

---

31. Movement for the Survival of the Ogoni People, *Ogoni Bill of Rights, Presented to the Government and People of Nigeria, October 1990* (Port Harcourt, Nigeria: Saros International Publishers, 1992).

The Ogoni people will make representation to the World Bank and the International Monetary Fund to the effect that giving loans and credit to the Nigerian Government on the understanding that oil money will be used to repay such loans is to encourage the Nigerian Government to continue to dehumanize the Ogoni people and to devastate the environment and ecology of the Ogoni and other delta minorities among whom oil is found . . .

The Ogoni people will inform the United Nations and the Organisation of African Unity that the Nigerian Constitution and the actions of the power elite in Nigeria flagrantly violate the UN Declaration of Human Rights and the African Charter of Human and Peoples Rights; and that Nigeria in 1992 is no different from Apartheid South Africa.

Despite his confidence in the rule of law, Saro-Wiwa knew he was up against some of the most repressive forces in Nigeria: the military government and the oil companies. In November 1992, MOSOP issued an ultimatum to Shell and NNPC: "Pay back-rents and royalties and also compensation for land devastated by oil exploration and production activities, or leave." The companies promptly ignored the demand. In response, MOSOP leaders organized a massive grassroots resistance campaign. Fundraising, speaking tours, street protests, election boycotts, pipeline sabotage, and an eloquent public relations campaign in the independent press garnered widespread sympathy at home and abroad. For a brief time in 1993, Shell suspended its operations in Ogoni.

But not for long. Shell soon began surveilling MOSOP members. In May 1993, the government issued the Treason and Treasonable Offenses Decree. Secession became a treasonable offense punishable by death. And the line between secession and ethnic or regional self-determination was a fine one, apparently. Shell and the central government intended to characterize MOSOP's demands as the former so as to justify an assault on its leaders. Later that year, private security forces on Shell's payroll commenced systematic massacres on Ogoni villages. Over one thousand Ogoni were killed and twenty thousand were made refugees in the first two weeks of September 1993 alone. The conspirators blamed the nearby Andoni ethnic group.

In the midst of the assault on Ogoni, Shell and the military government of Sani Abacha conspired to assassinate prominent members of the Gokana Council of Chiefs and Elders. After the killings, Abacha's military administrator in the Niger Delta, Lieutenant Colonel Dauda Komo, instructed his security forces to move through Ogoni and root out Saro-Wiwa and other MOSOP leaders. They were arrested and framed for the assassinations.[32] Writing from prison to a sympathetic Irish comrade, Saro-Wiwa lamented in November 1994 that "Shell are finally

---

32. Okonta and Douglas, *Where Vultures Feast*, 117, 126–34.

succeeding it would appear, in shutting me up. But that will surely not be the end of the matter."[33]

After the arrests, Shell Nigeria's chief executive Brian Anderson arranged private meetings (May–June 1995) with Saro-Wiwa in Lagos. At the meetings, Anderson tried to convince him to call off the Ogoni campaign against Shell's environmental and human rights abuses. In exchange, Anderson would pressure Abacha to drop the murder charges. Saro-Wiwa, steadfast in his commitment to the Ogoni cause, declined.

Following a sham military tribunal, the Ogoni Nine, including Saro-Wiwa were hanged at the Port Harcourt jail on November 10, 1995. During the execution, antiriot police cordoned off the prison. The Ogoni Nine were buried in an unmarked grave. International condemnation proved utterly toothless. Western nations implemented meager restrictions on travel and the sale of military hardware. But an oil embargo or asset seizure—the two tactics that could have actually punished Abacha's government for its actions—never materialized. No international criminal proceedings followed either.[34]

The Ogoni struggle is instructive on several key points about the politics of oil in the last quarter of the twentieth century. First, it demonstrates the degree to which oil revenues tended to corrupt the institutions of newly independent states. This corruption resulted not from an absence of democratic will or know-how, but from a continuation of colonial rule through the production of oil. International oil companies like Shell may not have owned the territory on which they extracted oil, but the economic leverage they maintained over the Nigerian government gave them a sense of free reign in the Niger Delta. In 1965, the Ghanian President Kwame Nkrumah dubbed this postindependence phenomenon "neocolonialism."[35]

Second, the Ogoni challenge to Shell and to the authority of the central government demonstrated that control over energy infrastructure, including pipelines and wellheads, could at times force concessions. In 1993, the Ogoni uprising, which featured coordinated cutoffs of flows of oil, resulted, albeit briefly, in Shell's abandonment of the territory. In 1995, when Saro-Wiwa was in jail, he suspected that Shell may even have been willing to pressure General Abacha to grant the Ogoni self-rule and to deliver them half of the oil revenues.[36] The intentions never resulted

---

33. Ken Saro-Wiwa to Majella McCarron, November 22, 1994, in *Silence Would Be Treason: The Last Writings of Ken Saro-Wiwa*, ed. Íde Corley, Helen Fallon, and Laurence Cox (Dakar, Senegal: Council for the Development of Social Science Research in Africa, 2013), 98.

34. Karl Maier, *This House Has Fallen: Midnight in Nigeria* (New York: Public Affairs, 2000), 109; Okonta and Douglas, *Where Vultures Feast*, 126–34.

35. Kwame Nkrumah, *Neo-Colonialism: The Last Stage of Imperialism* (New York: International Publishers, 1965), ix–xiii.

36. Ken Saro-Wiwa to Majella McCarron, September 14, 1995, in *Silence Would Be Treason*, 129.

FIGURE 5.3 "A Long Way After Botticelli"
Source: Martin Rowson, Graphic for "Unloveable Shell, the Goddess of Oil," article by Andrew Rowell, *The Guardian*, November 15, 1997.

in concrete change, but Shell was at some point sufficiently worried about the potential international blowback from its treatment of the Ogoni.

Third, the Ogoni experience reveals the degree to which international energy companies were willing to deploy violence against local populations that stood in their way. The collusion between the Nigerian government and Shell coupled with Shell's use of private mercenary security forces against the Ogoni exposed the painful reality that extraction—of not just carbon energy but other kinds of natural resources—tends toward violence in the absence of any proper accountability. As the British cartoonist Martin Rowson captured two years later (see Figure 5.3), Shell was never put on trial for its use of violence against the Ogoni. Instead Saro-Wiwa and the other MOSOP nine paid the ultimate price for speaking out against those crimes.

The rise of MOSOP coincided with another watershed in the history of carbon energy: the breakup of the Union of Soviet Socialist Republics (USSR). Almost overnight, fifteen new independent states emerged. Control of all of that oil that the Soviets marketed to Western Europe in the 1950s was potentially up for grabs. The largest American and British energy companies chomped at the bit.

But where to begin? And how to proceed? Eleven of the fifteen former Soviet republics possessed oil and gas potential.[37] Before the official dissolution of the

37. Gregory F. Ulmishek and Charles D. Masters, "Oil, Gas Resources Estimated in Former Soviet Union," *Oil and Gas Journal* 91, no. 50 (1993), https://www.ogj.com/articles/print/volume-91/issue-50/in-this-issue/exploration/oil-gas-resources-estimated-in-the-former-soviet-union.html.

USSR in December 1991, it was unclear to Western oil executives whether or not the Soviet Oil Ministry would entertain partnerships or investments.

Over the previous three years Soviet Premier Mikhail Gorbachev had made remarkable strides in democratizing the previously totalitarian Soviet system in response to sustained popular uprising. He'd freed the press. Citizens elected the president and vice president, as well as representatives to parliament and local councils. In economics, Gorbachev pursued social democracy—"a mixture of a free market and a strong safety net, with key industries under public control."[38] But his vision for a new Soviet society coincided with national independence movements throughout the USSR. Unless in pursuit of Russian oil fields, energy executives hedged that they'd eventually negotiate with new heads of state rather than Moscow.

Two Soviet republics in particular caught their attention. Azerbaijan flanked the western shore of the Caspian Sea. Kazakhstan extended from the Caspian's northeast coast some 1800 miles to China's far western border. Both possessed substantial oil fields. Azerbaijan had been the site of the Russian Empire's first big oil boom in the nineteenth century. The capital city of Baku had been a critical site of the revolutionary uprising of 1905 against Tsar Nicholas II, described in chapter 3. Under Soviet rule (1922–1991), Azeri oil played a crucial role in the USSR's planned industrialization, reaching peak production in 1969. But by the late 1980s lack of investment left the fields a shell of their former glory.[39]

Outplayed in Kazakhstan by its rival Chevron, BP focused on Azerbaijan, where a war with neighboring Armenia over a disputed border region called Nagorno-Karabakh was draining the coffers of the nationalist Popular Front that had come to power after the fall of the Soviet Union. In a set of negotiations that saw BP fly former British Prime Minister Margaret Thatcher to Baku to personally bargain with the State Oil Company of Azerbaijan (SOCAR), BP handed over a $30 million down payment for the rights to produce oil and build an export pipeline. Though ultimately unsuccessful in the war, the cash infusion helped the Azeri government sustain its conflict with Armenia that resulted in the displacement of over one million people from Nagorno-Karabakh.

Then in late 1993, the Popular Front was overthrown in a coup and Heydar Aliyev came to power. The former KGB agent and head of the Communist Party of Azerbaijan had been stripped of his Soviet credentials following a string of corruption charges and for his opposition to Gorbachev's reforms in the late 1980s. Ever the savvy political operator, Aliyev sided with nationalists following a Soviet massacre of 100 civilians in Baku in January 1990. Against the backdrop of the threat

---

38. Naomi Klein, *The Shock Doctrine: The Rise of Disaster Capitalism* (New York: Picador, 2007), 276.

39. Steven LeVine, *The Oil and the Glory: The Pursuit of Empire and Fortune on the Caspian Sea* (New York: Random House, 2007), 8–9; Marriott and Minio-Paluello, *The Oil Road*, 20–21.

of civil war and military battles with neighboring Armenia, Aliyev outmaneuvered his political opponents to secure the presidency.

Aliyev knew that if his family was to stand a chance of ruling for any length of time, he would need full control of Azeri oil. In particular, he worried about Russia reasserting its political influence. But Aliyev's first move seemed counterintuitive. Soon after his election, he canceled the contract that Thatcher had helped negotiate, sending BP and other oil companies back to the drawing board.[40]

But Aliyev was quick to secure a more favorable set of arrangements. He named his son Ilham second in command at SOCAR, and in 1994, Ilham led negotiations for the so-called Contract of the Century. Hashed out in Houston, Texas, Azeri negotiators recalled that "we had clear instructions from our president not to return empty-handed from the United States."[41] Amoco emerged with the majority share of the contract. When BP, initially a secondary operator in the Baku deal, bought Amoco in 1998, it assumed the role of chief operator.

By 1995, Aliyev's political goals coincided with those of Amoco, BP, and US President Bill Clinton: curb Russian influence. Russia and Iran protested the contract as a violation of its territorial rights over the Caspian Sea. Aliyev's negotiators had allegedly signed away oil concessions that were not theirs. A power struggle in Clinton's cabinet ensued over how to approach post–Cold War diplomacy with Russia. The hardliners won out, and they identified Azeri oil as a "strategic interest" worth American protection. Aliyev had his patron. The Cold War proper, barely four years gone, ramped back up.[42]

The focus turned to transport. Russia proposed an "Early Oil" plan to run oil through its existing pipeline network. Moscow hoped that the convenience and economic favorability would delay the construction of an alternate route. A plan to run a pipeline through the Republic of Georgia to the Black Sea was rumored to cost $250 million. Surely Amoco/BP would choose the Russian option.

Moscow was wrong. Clinton's deputy national security advisor Sandy Berger and the Republic of Georgia's President Eduard Shevardnadze convinced BP to build the Baku-Supsa pipeline. This was BP's chance to take control of Caspian oil. Its lawyers drafted and secured signatures on Host Government Agreements. They created the legal framework that allowed BP to construct and operate the pipeline "without having to amend local laws." In the words of BP's lawyer: "We went above or around them by using a treaty."[43]

---

40. Marriott and Minio-Paluello, *The Oil Road*, 57–59.

41. Khoshbakht Yussifzadeh quoted in Lutz Kleveman, *The New Great Game: Blood and Oil in Central Asia* (New York: Atlantic Monthly Press, 2003), 23.

42. Kleveman, *The New Great Game*, 24–25; Levine, *The Oil and the Glory*, 199–216.

43. George Goolsby, quoted in Marriott and Minio-Paluello, *The Oil Road*, 144.

In 1999, Clinton and the presidents of Georgia, Azerbaijan, Turkey, and Kazakhstan signed off on the Baku-Tbilisi-Ceyhan pipeline, which ran oil from the Caspian southwest to the Turkish Mediterranean port near the Syrian border. A similar set of legal arrangements ensured that the BTC pipeline avoided pesky local concerns about property ownership, environmental damage, and taxation. The citizens of the countries along the pipeline routes had little recourse with their own national governments, which had signed away a great deal of authority and control to BP.[44]

What does the Contract of the Century teach us about the politics of carbon energy at the twentieth century's end? First, it demonstrates that despite the breakup of the Soviet Union in 1991, the Cold War rivalry kindled at the end of World War II remained a powerful force in world politics. Initially the United States emerged from the Cold War with designs to seriously engage with Russia. But by the end of Clinton's first term, his advisors had revived the "Great Game" strategies of the late nineteenth century that featured Britain and Russia locked in shrewd struggles over the resources of Central Asia without regard for the people that lived there. As one Azeri farmer exclaimed in early 2002, she would rather be forced to move and receive compensation from the Aliyev government than to face down what was planned: the tunneling of the BTC pipeline underneath her home. "If the pipeline burns," she warned, "I'll burn with it."[45]

Second, as in Nigeria, oil extraction relied on undemocratic rule in Azerbaijan, Georgia, and other states through which oil pipelines passed. Heydar Aliyev, who died in 2003 and was succeeded by his son Ilham, was president of a nominal democracy. But it was one with extremely weak civil and legal checks on the president. Aliyev was beholden to foreign energy companies for the state's budget. In that sense, Azeris had merely traded one foreign power (the Soviet Union) for another (BP). The weakening or thwarting of democracy that had begun in the Middle East at the hands of SoCal and BP during the early Cold War continued largely unabated after the Cold War's end.

In the conclusion, we turn to North America, where indigenous people have put themselves on the front lines of the fight against carbon energy projects that threaten the planet's survival in the twenty-first century. But while our collective struggle to keep the planet's atmosphere livable may be relatively new, First Nations in Canada and Native Americans in the United States are engaged in a centuries-old battle against industrial capitalism that intensified with the dawn of the carbon age.

---

44. Levine, *The Oil and the Glory*, 356–57.

45. Quoted in Marriott and Minio-Paluello, *The Oil Road*, 103.

FURTHER READING

Jones, Toby Craig. "America, Oil, and War in the Middle East." *Journal of American History* 99, no. 1 (June 2012): 208–18.

LeVine, Steven. *The Oil and the Glory: The Pursuit of Empire and Fortune on the Caspian Sea.* New York: Random House, 2007.

Marriott, James, and Mika Minio-Paluello. *The Oil Road: Journeys from the Caspian Sea to the City of London.* New York: Verso, 2013.

Okonta, Ike, and Oronto Douglas. *Where Vultures Feast: Shell, Human Rights, and Oil in the Niger Delta.* San Francisco: Sierra Club Books, 1992.

Parra, Francisco. *Oil Politics: A Modern History of Petroleum.* London: I. B. Tauris, 2004.

Sabin, Paul. "Crisis and Continuity in U.S. Oil Politics, 1965–1980." *Journal of American History,* 99, no. 1 (June 2012): 177–86.

CONCLUSION

Protest Energy

> We are the earth and sky
> We are the thunder cries
> We are the fire,
> We are the light in your eyes
> We are standing strong
> Like a rock, like a stone
> On this sacred ground we belong
> We are home
>
> —SARA THOMSEN, *"Mni Wičoni (Water is Life)"* 2017

Winona LaDuke lives and works on the White Earth Indian Reservation in northern Minnesota. A Native American rights activist since the American Indian Movement (AIM) of the 1970s, she has applied her social justice experience to the twinned problems of climate change and economic inequality. In December 2018, she articulated a vision for what she and others call an Indigenous Green New Deal—a radical economic shift away from fossil-fueled global systems of production and consumption to largely self-sustaining localized economies powered by renewable energy.

Winona's Hemp and Heritage Farm, begun in 2017, is proof of concept for what this new economy can look like: self-sustaining, educational, generational. "To be honest with you . . . I didn't really like this [carbon] economy too much. Didn't work out too well for my people [American Indians], you know. So the next economy has to be something that reaffirms our relationship to the Earth and gives us a shot," LaDuke said in 2018. But LaDuke's Ojibwe, like other indigenous people around the world, are up against the economic and political power of the fossil fuel industry.[1]

---

1. "Winona LaDuke Calls for Indigenous-led 'Green New Deal' as She Fights Minnesota Pipeline Expansion," *Democracy Now!*, December 7, 2018, https://www.democracynow.org/2018/12/7/winona_laduke_calls_for_indigenous_led.

At an estimated 1.6 trillion barrels, Alberta, Canada's Athabasca Oil Sands (tar sands), comprise the world's largest reserve of recoverable heavy crude (bitumen) and third largest oil reserve overall behind Venezuela and Saudi Arabia. About 20 percent of the tar sands requires surface mining rather than drilling because the oil is mixed in with sand, clay, and water no more than 70 meters below the surface. The process involves the razing of boreal forest that sits atop the oil. The remaining 80 percent of recoverable reserves demands hydraulic fracturing (fracking), the same method required to extract gas. Both methods use copious amounts of water, much of which ends up in toxic tailing ponds, both above ground and under, where the waste poisons aquifers.

Global Forest Watch reported that from 2000 to 2013, tar sands mining resulted in the razing of 775,000 hectares of boreal forest, with habitat disruption estimated at 12.5 million hectares.[2] In terms of deforestation, Athabasca makes oil production in Mexico's Huasteca rainforest in the early twentieth century look like child's play. Once extracted, the bitumen is so heavy that it must be mixed with solvents in order to flow through pipelines. If spilled in waterways, it sinks, making it extraordinarily difficult to clean up.

Of course, the land-locked tar sands are only profitable if energy companies can get it to market. To this end, over the last decade, they have proposed and begun to build a web of export pipelines running west to Pacific coast terminals for export to Asia, east to the populous provinces of Quebec and New Brunswick, and south across the US border to the Gulf of Mexico, where US energy companies can refine the heavy crude into usable forms. In 2015, four major pipeline projects formed the nucleus of this tar sands export scheme: Northern Gateway (Enbridge), Energy East (TC Energy), Keystone XL (TC Energy), and Trans Mountain (Kinder Morgan). The companies have sought state, provincial, and national regulatory approval in both the United States and Canada to build and operate these pipelines. They have frequently attempted to have local and national governments invoke eminent domain, a legal device used to strip property from private owners in order to build infrastructure that is in theory supposed to serve the public interest (think the government kicking you out of your house to build a highway through your neighborhood).

This is where the economic interests of the dozen or so energy companies with stakes in Alberta tar sands collides with the political will of indigenous communities in both the United States and Canada, including LaDuke's Ojibwe. Let us take for example Enbridge's Northern Gateway pipeline, which the company first announced in 2006. While the Canadian government's regulatory process remains rather stringent, Canada's National Energy Board is dominated by

2. Rachel Petersen, Nigel Sizer, and Peter Lee, "Tar Sands Threaten World's Largest Boreal Forest," blog, *Global Forest Watch*, July 15, 2014, https://blog.globalforestwatch.org/supplychain/tar-sands-threaten-worlds-largest-boreal-forest.

members who formerly worked in the oil and gas industry. This revolving door scenario has, in the minds of many experts, meant that the best legal challenge to the expansion of tar sands pipelines rests with Section 35 of the Canadian constitution. Enshrined in 1982, Section 35 mandates a "duty to consult and, if appropriate, to accommodate the concerns of Indigenous peoples" in cases where their rights and well being may be adversely impacted by the government's actions. These include approval of energy infrastructure projects like pipelines, power plants, or hydroelectric dams.

But court challenges are expensive and unpredictable. In many cases, one lawyer suspects, the Canadian government simply goes through the motions of consultation and ignores the substance of indigenous concerns, all with reasonable expectation that a judge will later rule the proposed project can proceed because the government's representatives—who are often employed by the energy industry—completed the mandatory consult.[3] To that end, First Nations in Canada, as well as their counterparts in the United States, are not putting all of their eggs into the proverbial legal basket. Instead, they are on the front lines, actively blocking pipeline construction.

The Unist'ot'en clan, part of the Wet'suwet'en First Nation, is leading one such resistance movement. Since at least 2008, the clan has been physically blockading no fewer than ten pipeline projects proposed to run through Wet'suwet'en territory in British Columbia. They have blockaded bridges and created checkpoints to prevent company surveying crews from planning routes, torn out route markers if found on hereditary lands, and built action camps, cabins, pit houses, permaculture gardens, and other infrastructure directly in the route of proposed pipelines. "I'm occupying our homeland," says Freda Huson, a Unist'ot'en spokesperson, who hopes that the movement will inspire others to return to the territory and engage older ways of living. "We're asserting our rights on our lands, and we're not breaking any laws. We're doing what our ancestors would have done," says Toghestiy, an Unist'ot'en hereditary chief.[4] In the absence of a favorable court ruling that kills the pipeline projects, the Unist'ot'en resolve that their continued resistance through blockade will delay the pipelines in perpetuity and cause financial investors to pull out, effectively killing the projects. This worked in 2016, when Enbridge canceled the Northern Gateway pipeline. But in 2018, a Canadian court did hand down an unfavorable ruling. In response, TC Energy enlisted the Canadian Royal Mounted Police to enforce the injunction against the Wet'suwet'en, which had been

---

3. Christopher Curtis, "In the Pipelines' Path: Canada's First Nations Lead Resistance," *Montreal Gazette*, September 8, 2015, https://montrealgazette.com/news/pipeline-resistance.

4. EJOLT Films, "Corridors of Resistance: Stopping Oil and Gas Pipelines," directed by Leah Temper, 2015, YouTube, https://youtu.be/ZDR1l_Xw7ts.

successfully blocking the company's Coastal GasLink pipeline project. In February 2020, Police raided the resistance camps and arrested the tribal matriarchs.[5]

Similar resistance efforts in eastern Canada and in the United States have hampered and delayed construction efforts on the Energy East, Dakota Access, and Line 3 pipelines. Near the Standing Rock Sioux reservation in North Dakota, an alliance organized and led by Lakota Sioux youth calling themselves "water protectors" swelled to form the Oceti Sakowin camp that in 2016 blocked the Dakota Access pipeline route. The water protectors pressured US President Barack Obama, after much dithering, to deny approval of the pipeline. This was not before North Dakota state police and private security forces hired by the pipeline company attacked water protectors with German shepherds and fire hoses. The footage evoked comparisons to Birmingham, Alabama in 1963, when racist cops and vigilantes violently attacked African Americans in order to maintain segregation and voter suppression.

In keeping with the growing resistance, in 2017, members of LaDuke's Ojibwe locked themselves to equipment to stop construction of Enbridge's Line 3 pipeline in Minnesota.[6] "Indeed an alliance of indigenous nations, from coast to coast, is being formed against all the pipeline, rail and tanker projects that would make possible the continued expansion of tar sands," writes Serge Simon, Mohawk Kanesatake Grand Chief, who is active in attempts to block the Energy East pipeline project in Quebec.[7]

What do we make of these efforts by indigenous people and allies to stop flows of North American oil in the twenty-first century? On the one hand, we could see these more recent events as unique, given the sheer magnitude and urgency of the global climate crisis. If the crisis is unprecedented, then their actions must be. Moreover, we could see the Unist'ot'en, Ojibwe, Lakota Sioux, Mohawk, and others as the vanguard of the global climate justice movement that seeks to sweep away coal and oil in favor of solar, wind, and geothermal energy. Maybe some see themselves that way too.

But I would argue that while the climate crisis is unprecedented in its scale, indigenous activists are firmly within the historical tradition of political resistance to carbon-fueled industrial capitalism and colonialism. With obvious connections

---

5. Alleen Brown and Amber Bracken, "No Surrender: After Police Defend a Gas Pipeline Over Indigenous Land Rights, Protesters Shut Down Railway's Across Canada," *The Intercept*, February 23, 2020, https://theintercept.com/2020/02/23/wetsuweten-protest-coastal-gaslink-pipeline/.

6. Audrea Lim, "'The Next Standing Rock': Minnesota's Indigenous Water Protectors are already Camping to Defeat Line 3," *The Progressive*, December 2017/January 2018, 18–20.

7. Laura Pedersen, "Mohawks threaten to block Energy East pipeline, saying project is threat to way of life," *National Post*, March 14, 2016, https://nationalpost.com/news/canada/mohawks-threaten-to-block-energy-east-pipeline-saying-project-is-threat-to-way-of-life.

to the Ogoni of Nigeria, today's water protectors and pipeline blockaders also reflect the aspirations of sixteenth-century English peasants whose common lands were privatized for the coal that lay beneath. Likewise, they carry on the quests for greater democratic participation that pervaded the coal mines, oil fields, and rail yards of early twentieth-century Essen, Baku, and Ludlow. Further, they are standing up to the same economic and political power of the international oil industry that propped up repressive governments in Iran, Iraq, and Saudi Arabia during and after the Cold War.

But the lesson here is not that history inevitably repeats itself. Rather, it is that at this critical juncture, there are useful historical precedents and strategies that can remake the politics of carbon energy anew.

In this book, I have tried to offer a model of research into the historical roots of an urgent contemporary issue—carbon energy—the burning of which continues to warm the planet. I have in no way been comprehensive (no historian ever truly is), but have instead built my arguments on a series of case studies and organized them chronologically to show how the politics of carbon energy has changed over time, even if some aspects seem to have changed little (the profit motive, for example). My sincerest intention, as I stated in the introduction, is that this volume helps to spark further research, debate, and curiosity. I have left holes in the story, and there are places and times that I did cover, but with specific questions in mind that led me to move past equally important developments.

Take for example the very brief case study presented in this conclusion: indigenous resistance to the further expansion of North America's carbon infrastructure in the twenty-first century. My coverage of the topic only spans about ten years. But to be sure, with an intriguing set of research questions and the skills to seek out, organize, and make sense of historical sources, this conclusion alone could transform into a book-length research project that explores the case of indigenous resistance in deep historical perspective. Now, my suspicion is that most of you do not intend to write a book on the subject. But the main difference between a short historical essay and a book-length treatment is word count, not necessarily effectiveness.

Let's wrap up by considering possible research questions—often the next step once you've identified and learned about a contemporary issue of importance (note the recent news articles I have cited here). I don't recommend trying to tackle all of these. A robust list can always be pared down:

- When and how did indigenous groups first respond to the first large-scale carbon projects in North America?
- Let's take coal for example, the nineteenth century's primary carbon fuel. How did American Indians and First Nations in Canada respond to the expansion of coal mining and railroads? How did those responses change over time and why?

- What about oil? How did indigenous groups negotiate the rise of oil in the twentieth century?
- Indigenous groups are wildly diverse. In what ways were their responses diverse as well? Did most groups resist? Did some collaborate? What considerations might individuals, families, and communities have faced in the growing carbon economy?
- Were there important historical differences between the United States and Canada that in turn shaped the range of possibilities available to indigenous people living within the borders of those nations?
- Both the United States and Canada are white settler colonies, previously part of the British Empire. Were historical developments there similar to other white settler colonies (say South Africa, Australia, or New Zealand as examples) with regards to indigenous populations and carbon extraction? If so, how? If not, why not?

Once you have a list of possible research questions, narrowing it down can be tricky. You can choose your favorite one, but the potential unavailability of sources may lead you down a dead end. I often begin by seeking out book-length coverage that is intentionally broad and that is pitched to an educated but nonspecialist readership. Once you have a handle on the larger historical periods and changes that have shaped, for example First Nations' experiences in Canada, you can begin to narrow your search by adding in more search terms: coal *or* oil *and* . . . wait for it . . . history!

The search engine experience is often trial and error. You'll come out of it with some useful books and articles but more importantly the experience to be more effective with your search the next time. And there will be a next time. And new or refined questions. One source will point you to others that never appeared in your search. Rather than a linear process that moves along a straight line, research often involves side trips and backtracking but ultimately growth. Stick with it. You'll be wiser for the time.

INDEX

ABOUT THE COVER

The cover image depicts Native Americans gathered along Highway 1806 near Cannonball, North Dakota on August 15, 2016. That year, indigenous communities organized resistance camps along the proposed route for the Dakota Access Pipeline. Denied necessary permitting by Barack Obama in late 2016 after police attacked protestors with German shepherds and water cannons, Donald Trump approved the pipeline in 2017. It carries oil from the Bakken oil fields in northwest North Dakota, under the Missouri River en route to an oil terminal in Illinois. In late 2019, Energy Transfer Partners, the pipeline's operator, sought to double the capacity of the pipeline, increasing the chances of drinking water contamination for millions of people. Wet plate collodion photograph by Shane Balkowitsch.